Maid of Sark

by
SIBYL HATHAWAY
Dame of Sark

ILLUSTRATED

Color plates from paintings of Sark by
J. M. W. TURNER

D. APPLETON-CENTURY COMPANY
INCORPORATED
New York   1939   *London*

PRINTED IN THE UNITED STATES OF AMERICA

Printing Statement:

Due to the very old age and scarcity of this book,
many of the pages may be hard to read due to the
blurring of the original text, possible missing pages,
missing text and other issues beyond our control.

Because this is such an important and rare work, we
believe it is best to reproduce this book regardless of
its original condition.

Thank you for your understanding.

La Coupée

By J. M. W. TURNER

To

MONSIEUR PIERRE PANNIER

whose interest in the Island
prompted this story

I *am deeply indebted to* MONSIEUR PIERRE PANNIER *who allowed me to draw freely upon his time and assistance for the original French text of this story, and to my niece,* CYNTHIA HATHAWAY, *for her friendly aid in this English translation.*—S. H.

Here earth lies lordly, triumphal as heaven is above her
And splendid and strange as the sea that upbears as an
    ark,
As a sign for the rapture of storm-spent eyes to discover,
Sark.

A. C. SWINBURNE

ILLUSTRATIONS

✎ FOREWORD ✎

The Feudal Island of Sark

THE Anglo-Norman Channel Islands are called
Jersey, Guernsey, Alderney, Sark, and Herm, and
with their countless reefs they seem the last remain-
ing traces of a giant's path now half-lost in the sea
across the Bay of St. Malo.

Jersey, the largest and the most southerly of the
islands, must once, according to an old map found at
the Abbey of Montebourg, have formed part of the
Cotentin. In the sixth century the Bishop of Coutances
made his episcopal visits there by crossing a plank
over a narrow brook. But little by little the brook grew
wider and deeper, until at last it became an arm of
the sea, and a later bishop had to give permission to

the inhabitants of Ecréhou (small islands, now deserted, half-way between Jersey and the Continent) to build a church of their own, since they could no longer go on foot to hear Mass at Carteret, their parish church.

Further north, Guernsey was once a part of what are now the islands of Jethou and Herm, and Alderney reached to the reefs of the Casquets.

Thus the Channel Islands are truly what Victor Hugo called them: "bits of French earth fallen into the sea and gathered up by England."

But while their people are always sincere in their allegiance to the English Crown, they never forget their Norman origin, nor England's conquest in 1066 at the hands of their Norman duke, William the Conqueror. Very tenacious as they are of their liberties and privileges, it is as Duke of Normandy that they render homage to the English king. Their speech is still the old Norman patois, and albeit all of them speak English to-day, most of them talk among themselves in the dialect of their forefathers.

Sercq, which the English call Sark, has six hundred inhabitants. It is three and a half miles long and about a mile and a half wide. With its high rugged cliffs which drop away sharply into the sea, it is reminiscent, like its name, of a sarcophagus. Only in Sark of all the Islands is there so marked a contrast between the wild coast-line and the calm and pleasant land it incloses, as great as the medieval contrast between pillaging Bretons and farming Normans. The complete absence of reptiles—neither snakes nor toads are to be found there—leads one to think that Sark must have been early separated from the other Islands and from the Cotentin. It consists of three parts—the smallest, Brecqhou, is separated from Great Sark by a narrow strip of sea, while Great Sark is joined to Little Sark by only an extraordinary natural causeway, thirteen feet wide and two hundred yards long, sloping on each side sharply down to the sea, a dizzying two hundred and forty feet below. This is called the "Coupée" and annually attracts many tourists. Near the eastern tip of the Island, surmounted by a modern lighthouse whose siren screams dolefully from time to time through fog, is the port called the Creux Harbor, surely the smallest in the world, whose sheer bluffs and narrow tunnel, the only way to the interior of the Island, always astound visitors. Next to this tunnel is another which could only be used at low tide, and where once a portcullis was in use for protection against enemies.

Though there are four hotels in Sark and forty farms, there is really no town; the Seigneurie, the parish church, the tiny post-office, the schools, and the recreation-hall are not even grouped together, so that the fields alternate with flower gardens all over the Island. There are many wells and brooks, and since frost is very rare, from February onwards it is a mass of wild flowers. For a long time the Island was believed to be infested with a malicious type of witches who entered houses by way of the chimney at night, so the old houses were always provided with a projecting stone slab at the base of every chimney to offer a resting-place to the witch in the hope that she would sit there and leave the interior of the house alone. Luckily the witches have disappeared, but the stones are still to be seen.

With its miniature parliament of fifty-two members, called the Chief Pleas—practically one representative for every ten people, including women and children—Sark might be considered the smallest democracy in the world. She is not represented in Westminster nor does English law apply, because actually, in law, the Island remains a feudal state, and the Dame of Sark continues to pay her duty of one-twentieth of a knight's fee to the Crown, a duty fixed

The Coupée—"thirteen feet wide and two hundred yards long"
By J. M. W. TURNER

in 1565 by Queen Elizabeth. Every tenant continues in his obligation to be ready with his musket to come to the defense of the Island in case of attack.

These tenants are the descendants of the forty families who went to Sark with the first Seigneur, Sir Helier de Carteret. Their lands pass from eldest son to eldest son, and with the land the right to a vote in the Chief Pleas.

Three times a year, at St. Michael's Day, at Easter, and at Christmas, the Seneschal posts a notice on the parish church door to call together the Chief Pleas in the little school-room where they learned to read as children. Their meetings never take very long, for their chief purpose is the upholding of tradition, and their decisions are always unanimous. They vote on the budget, prepared by a committee of twelve members—the Douzainiers—and elect for one year a Vingtenier, who becomes a Constable the following year. Both are charged to see that the law is maintained. The Seneschal metes out justice—the Provost executes it.

The Seneschal orders punishments up to twice twenty-four hours of imprisonment and fines of two pounds. For serious crimes the offender is sent before the Royal Court of Guernsey, but for minor offenses

he is often let go with an admonition to behave himself in the future. In the case of any person not of
Sark birth, he may be required to leave the Island
immediately and forever.

In civil cases there still exists the "Clameur de
Haro," a solemn protest made before witnesses and
followed by the recitation of the Lord's Prayer, which
instantly suspends all action until the complaint has
been brought before the Court.

The Seneschal applies the old civil laws enacted by
the Chief Pleas and the Seigneur himself is bound by
the laws which he himself has approved in the parliament, except for certain privileges which allow him,
for instance, to shoot over any land on the Island
without being questioned or disturbed, to own a mill
where the tenants may have their wheat ground, and
a pigeon cote where he alone may keep pigeons, and
to be the sole owner of a female dog on the Island
(because in 1696 a bitch with puppies severely bit the
daughter of the then Seigneur) ; all property to which
there is no heir within the fifth degree of affinity re-
verts to him; and, finally, he has a right of veto over
any of the enactments of the Chief Pleas.

It is forbidden at all times under pain of heavy fine
to shoot sea-gulls, because of their assistance to sailors

in foggy weather, indicating by their raucous cries the proximity of rocks and dangerous reefs. On the other hand, there is a reward given for the destruction of the cormorants who are ravenous fish-eaters.

The Sabbath is strictly observed as a day of rest, and only twelve visitors are allowed by law to land from any commercial boat on Sunday. All inhabitants are to drive a cart or carriage save in case of actual necessity—of course, this does not apply to automobiles, for they are never allowed on the Island under any circumstances. The carriages which transport tourists are far from modern, but they make up in picturesqueness for what they lack in comfort.

The salaries of the officials already mentioned are provided for out of the budget, but the Constable and the Vingtenier receive no recompense, and have as their sole symbol of authority a small square baton. They are authorized to ascertain that the wine, beer, and cider for sale in the hotels and taverns are unadulterated, and they collect the small property tax, which they hand over to another unpaid official, the Collecteur des Pauvres, who is responsible for apportioning public assistance to those in need through age or infirmity. The only other paid officials are the Vicar, the Doctor, the Schoolmaster and Schoolmistress, and the Grave-digger. There is no income tax, but the old corvée still exists which obliges every man over sixteen years of age to give two days a year unpaid labor to the upkeep of the roads, for which, however, a substitute may be hired.

There is no industry in Sark, and yet there is no unemployment or want; the income of the people is from fishing, agriculture, and tourists. During the last century an attempt was made to renew the working of some old silver mines on the Island, but this was abandoned owing to inundations by the sea.

It is hard to believe that this peaceful Island whose people seem to lead an ideally happy existence was once the scene of so many invasions and such frightful massacres that its inhabitants were more than once forced to desert it, after vain attempts to hide there, and that for many years it was believed to be the object of a curse.

Because of its double girdle of dangerous rocks and precipitous cliffs, Sark was an impregnable stronghold for those marauders who were powerful enough to take it. There are still many traces of crumbling walls and earthworks of old forts constructed by French invaders, and old cannon still lie on the cliffs half hidden in gorse and bracken. All the scum of the Channel tried at various times in the Middle Ages to settle there, and it was very difficult to get rid of them except by famine or trickery. It was not until 1565 when Queen Elizabeth made it a Seigneurie, which she granted by charter to Sir Helier de Carteret of Jersey, that the Island ceased to be a source of trouble and unrest in the Channel. At that time Sark had been entirely deserted.

The Charter of 1565 continues in force in the Island, and the flag which floats from the Seigneurie tower on festival days is still the same—a red cross on a white ground, with two leopards passant in the upper quarter.

❧ I ❧

NIGHTFALL, in the month of May, 1565. From their little boat Gilles, the fisherman, and his three young companions, two of them his sons and the other Lucas the Minstrel, watched the western sun as it sank deeper and deeper into the sea behind Herm and Guernsey, while, in the east, the steep bluffs of Sark, leaden at the base and crimson at their summit, seemed a great funeral couch, covered with a purple cloth.

The wind scarcely filled the great sail, and the four men, anxious to scale the rocks before dark, began to row more determinedly. They pulled away with all their strength, keeping time to a song, sad as a prayer for the dead, in which their voices took up the words, one after the other:

"In Coutances in Normandy,
St. Elias and St. Hilary,
Kneeling pious, raise their plea
To Mary Virgin, our Lady.

"Beg her blessing on this land
Of Sark, which in days out of mind—
Pray for us!—from out the deep,
Druids' curse did know and keep.

"Miserere mei."

"Is it true, Father," one of Gilles's sons asked him, "that the ground of Sark is accursed, as they say?"

"It must be, son. I remember my father told it me often, when I was no more than a little lad clinging to his coat-tails. Long years ago, our ancestors followed the priests of another faith; the Druids, they were called. In their ceremonies, those priests used to sacrifice young girls upon their great stone altars—you have seen their like often at Jersey.

"When St. Magloire drove them out, the Druids uttered a frightful prophecy on the people of the land: 'For ten centuries, the women and girls of this island will be ravished by foreign invaders.' But they could not alarm the good Saint, for he gave them tit for tat. 'The day will come,' he said, 'when one of those girls, as lovely as she is pure, will be beloved with a hopeless love by a lord from a land which the sun lights even as it sets here. And from that day forward, the folk of Sark will live forevermore in peace and happiness.' "

As they listened again to the familiar words of the legend, Jerome's and Hyacinthe's dreams turned to their own dear acquaintances, Corisande and Douce-Marie, Lucas' sisters. And Lucas, who was soon to marry Gilles's daughter Guillette, thought that she, too, was good and beautiful, but that it would displease him mightily for her to be loved, even hopelessly, by a stranger from that mysterious land.

"There can be no such island," they all murmured. "Only think how often we have sailed into the setting sun in search of it. But always sky and sea alone stretched out before us, to the unbroken line of the horizon."

"True enough," Gilles answered. "But it is true as well that we have had more than once to flee to the caves because Sark was being invaded by warriors who pillaged our houses, misused our daughters, and still were not satisfied in their wickedness. It was not so long ago that Buron and his ruffian Bretons put poor little Amice, and Fanchon, the pock-marked, and Marguerite, the roguish one, to death, after they had ravished them. And the nuns from the Convent, whom they carried away captive. Would it not be sad to think that we Normans were fated never to have revenge upon such swine?"

The little boat made its way between the rocks of the Grune and the Pêcheresse, and slid into calm water as it neared the tiny landing of the Éperquerie. Her passengers lowered the sail, and leaning more heavily upon their oars, took up again their melancholy song in the still shadows of dusk which lay over earth and sea. But Lucas, thinking that Guillette awaited him at the cliff's top, seized his mandore, and began with his wooden pick to draw forth notes which told more clearly and more sweetly than any words of his heart's tenderness and the ever-burning flame of his longing for her.

ᔥ II ᔥ

L IKE all the folk of Sark, Gilles was a farmer as
well as a fisherman.

In his little cottage, surrounded by a small field of
wheat, at the edge of the cliff overlooking the Éperquerie, his wife Catherine and Guillette, his daughter,
were busy laying the table for supper, a slice of bacon
and a goat cheese. In the fireplace, hanging from a
ring above the glowing embers, an iron pot held a fra-
grant soup. Guillette's happy smile showed her white
teeth, gleaming in the room's darkness. Leaning over
the hearth, she lit a tallow candle which she carried in
its wooden holder to the center of the table, and her
almost almond-shaped eyes, blue as the sea, shared
suddenly the smile of her strong full lips, moist as the
inside of a ripe fruit.

Curls framed her determined little face, appealing and disturbing in its beauty to the young men of the Island. Though she was still very young, her rounded throat, left bare by the loose fichu, rose from shoulders already plump above a firm, curved breast. She wore a jacket of garnet fustian, through which passed the lace-trimmed sleeves of her underblouse, and a bell-shaped skirt of the same color widened above her bare legs.

"I am very happy," she said to her mother. "Tomorrow is Whitsunday, and Father Samson will announce our betrothal before his sermon. After the procession there will be the party, and, if you allow, I shall stay until evening with Lucas and his sisters. I shall dance with Lucas as long as my legs will carry me, while my brothers court Douce-Marie and Corisande."

"Lucas the Minstrel is a fine boy," answered Catherine. "There is nothing to be said against him. But you are only a little girl, too young to marry, and I would that you wait till St. Magloire's Day for the wedding. The Saint will take especial care of you, if you are married on his day. . . . Guillette, will you watch the soup while I fetch a pitcher of cider from the cellar? Otherwise, the men will have plenty

A little cottage at the edge of the cliff

to eat but nothing to drink when they come in."

"Very well, I'll watch, but I'm sure that they are already passing the point. I can even hear them singing their landing-song that makes me sad only to listen to it," answered the girl, as the strains of their song floated up to her.

She stepped quickly to the threshold, then ran to the edge of the cliff, and her gentle voice blended with the men's song, while she sang a song she had made up herself to the tune of "Claire Fontaine," a song which told of her most secret longings:

> "In our flowering islands,
> More than one lass is fair,
> But the one whom I envy
> Is she who frees our land.
> Allelui, alleluia,
> Traderideri, traderidera."

"You are mad, little Guillette. What do you mean, my poor child, with your songs that make my blood run cold? Surely it is not you who will drive out the Bretons, if they come back? Do you sing that only to make me angry?"

But Guillette was already far away. Sitting at the edge of the cliff, with her feet dangling over, she had seized from its stake a long rope which stretched to the sea. Now, holding it between her hands, and crossing her legs over it, she slid down it to the rocks, just as the boat reached shore. Catching the mooring rope which Lucas threw her, she helped the men unload their catch of fish. Each began to gut his own eels with his knife, to hang them out on the racks where they would dry, the racks which had given the harbor of the Éperquerie its name.

Lucas and Guillette chatted gaily as they worked side by side, and Gilles and his sons watched them with affectionate smiles. When the last fish was stretched on the rack, the men, oars on their shoulders, began the slow climb up the path to the house, while the lovers hung back, hand in hand. Above the path, the doorway of the lighted cottage, its outlines darkened only by Catherine's silhouette, made a square of brilliance against the clear sky.

When they had reached the heights, Guillette followed her father and her brothers, while Lucas, with a kiss on her upturned cheek, turned regretfully towards his own home at the Fontaine Bay on Little Sark, where, since the death of his parents, he lived alone with his sisters.

❦ III ❦

NEXT day, Whitsunday, the Island was *en fête.*
The little chapel, dim with tarnished gold and
dark windows, was thronged with people in their
gayest clothes, Guillette in a large linen coif with
wide strings tied demurely under her rounded chin,
and a bright crimson shawl over her shoulders crossed
over her breast and tied at the back, the ends hanging
over her blue skirt. Not far away Corisande and
Douce-Marie watched her through the fringe of their
long blond lashes, their heads discreetly lowered, as
if they knew how to read the pious words from the
prayer-book they held so carefully before their faces
to hide their sly smiles at their dear friend, who was
soon to be their sister as well, when she blushed scarlet at the priest's betrothal words. "There is promise

of marriage between Lucas Albin Gabriel, son of
Lucas, and Demoiselle Guillonne Marie Elène, better
known as Guillette, daughter of Gilles the fisherman
and of Catherine his wife, who live at the Éperquerie,"
he announced in a solemn voice. "If no one offers just
reason why this marriage should not take place, it will
be celebrated at the feast of St. Magloire, next October. From to-day forward we beg the special blessing
of our Saint on these two young people."

Every one knelt then, as the organ notes rang out,
enriched by the voices of the faithful in their "Gloria
in excelsis Deo," and the worm-eaten statue of the
Saint was brought from the church on four sturdy
pairs of shoulders and carried around the field, while
the bells' song grew fainter.

In the middle of the meadow boards laid across
wine-casks made a stand for the musicians, already
busily tuning up their instruments. One of them
pressed his bass viol between his knees, another drew
his bow across the three cords of a rebec, and a third
practised trills on his hautboy. And all along the road
from the Monastery, filled with carts, the horses and
cattle who had been unhitched browsed through the
grass, stopping now and again to break the air with
a thin sharp neigh or the deep resonance of a bellow.

As soon as the Mass was over, every one hastened to find the young couple to congratulate them. Father Samson himself, accompanied by Brother Augustin, joined them. Some gathered outside the inn where Guillette's father was offering cider to all comers.

Already some of the young people were dancing the Dance of the Three Hats, a figure of eight for four performers. Father Samson sat down among the older women, among them Guillette's mother, on a bench near-by. "Ah, Father, what can we do for the Saint, so that he will take good care of our children? We're losing heart here in Sark with all these raids of brigands. We say our prayers right enough, but the good Saint has forgotten us. Tell us, Father, why did he let them steal his sacred body from us?"

"Five hundred years ago, daughter, the Monastery here was large and important, with sixty-two monks and a prior. Now Brother Augustin and I inhabit a mere corner of the ruins. The Sanctuary of St. Magloire was famous for its miracles, and every year hundreds of pilgrims came on his day to visit the shrine, and ask for his blessing. One evening at dusk four Breton monks came to the door of the Monastery— very humble and holy they were, too—and begged to be taken in. After a few days they impressed the

brotherhood so much by their piety and their humility
—see how deceitful they can be, those Bretons—that
they were permitted to spend a night in prayer before
the Shrine. Oh, there wasn't anything they longed for
so much as that—they would bless the names of the
brotherhood forever. Only, the next morning when
our monks went into the chapel—lo and behold, the
Shrine was open and the sacred relics gone. And those
holy, those humble Bretons—were half-way to Jersey.
Of course, our people tried to pursue them, but there
was such a tempest that they had to turn back."

"But, Father, why did the Saint allow all this?"

"He wished to test our faith, my child. That's the
only reason he lets us suffer so much from the depre-
dations of the wicked Buron."

While the women shuddered at this dread name,
and crossed themselves, murmuring to the Saint to
protect them, the young people continued to dance
more and more vigorously, now whirling in a dance
with three steps to each side. Then, their hands link-
ing each other's waists, they spun violently around
several times, and the fun was at its height.

And Lucas and Guillette, holding each other by
the hand, looked deep into one another's eyes, and
smiled at what they glimpsed there.

ᔥᔥ IV ᔥᔥ

THE cottage was gray with dawn. Guillette rose from the boxlike bed with its mattress of dried ferns, stretched her arms over her head, and began her day's work. She had no more than blown the logs on the hearth to flaming life, when, through the open door, she caught a glimpse of something which roused her curiosity at first, then made her blood turn to ice in her veins.

Against the pale half-light of morning she could see a black shape at anchor, so motionless that it seemed a phantom ship, an unknown vessel which must have touched these shores during the night. Gun barrels lined its sides and, as Guillette watched, horses were let down by ropes into the small boats drawn up alongside. And above all floated the hateful banner of Brittany, a golden ermine on a field of blue.

Guillette, frozen with terror, called out to her parents who hurried to the doorway, their anguished eyes taking in every detail of what was going on below, as fifty men and a dozen horses landed on the rocky cliff.

In the slanting sunlight the men's helmets glistened like gold, and the water caught the reflection of the scarlet streaks of dawn in the lightening sky, until it seemed that there were great smears of blood upon it to add to the menacing terror of the scene.

"We haven't an instant to lose," said Gilles, his voice tense. "Guillette, you must run to the Monastery, and tell Father Samson that the Bretons are here. He'll ring the tocsin. Then go find Lucas, and ask him to take you across to Guernsey; you can stay with our cousins the Belloiseaus over there. We will hide in the pigsty, and if they don't find us, we'll try to come across to Guernsey to-night, too."

Below them the Bretons had begun their long climb up the steep mountain path, their feet padding on the dirt like those of a flock of sheep. As Guillette kissed her family good-by, she could see the tips of their pikes, and as she set out at a run across to the Monastery, she could hear their guttural mutterings only a little way behind her.

At last, pausing for breath, she turned to look at her home, and saw sharp pink tongues of flame licking across the roof of thatch.

V

I T WAS not long before Guillette reached the Monastery woods, green with ash and holly, and leaped over a tiny pool, whose still waters, now broken only by water-lilies, had once driven the monks' mill. This was St. Magloire's fountain, and all the folk of the Island knew that one had but to whisper a wish into its depths for the Saint to hear and grant. Guillette scooped a drop or two of its water into her palms, as she knelt among the golden irises at its edge, and murmured, "Good Saint, grant that we will all be together again one day, and that Lucas and I will get married, and let all this be just a dreadful nightmare, and let me wake up by and by."

A bird as blue as the sky, a kingfisher, flew up with a sudden song from a clump of bracken beside her, and its zigzag flight to and fro across the pond brought new hope into her heart.

Guillette rattled the door in the granite wall, pushed it open, and went through cloisters, overgrown with bright weeds, to the Chapel of St. Eustace where she could hear Father Samson at his prayers. When she ran up to him and threw herself at his feet, the priest rose from his knees.

"Father, Father," Guillette sobbed, "the Bretons have come back. They are almost here."

"There, there, child. Calm yourself. Now tell me what you know about it."

"A ship has anchored at the Éperquerie, and the Bretons have landed. They've set fire to our house, and I've come to warn you, so that you could ring the bells."

The old man crossed himself, and whispered, "Into Thy hands, O Lord," as he looked sadly at the girl.

Suddenly there was a shadow across the sunlight at the door, and looking up the two saw a soldier on horseback, his armor glistening. Rising in his stirrups, he stared at the priest and the girl, through the split in his white-plumed vizor. His right hand held his horse's bridle, whilst his left rested upon the hilt of a long curved sword attached to his saddle.

Lifting his vizor he disclosed a nose as hooked as an owl's beak, even more alarming because of the gray mustaches which framed it, and the empty eye-socket which gave a particularly brutal look to his ugly face.

Cantering behind him came a young woman in green velvet, proudly erect in the side-saddle of her dun horse. Her honey-colored hair fell in ringlets from her scarlet cap, down over her forehead to her plucked eyebrows. Her thin nose, the flare of her nostrils, her blue eyes, her mocking painted lips, made her look wilful and sensual. Her red-trimmed white skirt was split to show white leather boots, and a small dagger hung from her golden girdle. A tiny gray monkey perched on the pommel of her saddle, and the hand which fondled it carelessly held a short, pliable switch. She halted just behind the leader, as three more horsemen drew up in back of her, the first holding a blue-and-gold banner, the others armed with blue-bannered lances. One of them wore a cornet at his shoulder. Their saddles were laden with sharp-pointed arms on one side, with broadswords in brown leather scabbards on the other.

"Is it you, Father, who govern the folk of this Island?" asked the leader hoarsely.

"God alone rules here, on earth as in Heaven," replied the priest.

"His will be done. Amen. But from to-day forward, I, Marc-Anthony Agénor Buron, Lord of Bruel and Marquis of Rosporden, called the Destroyer, I intend to be the sole instrument of His will. And here is the charming Princess Gaud, whom you will obey, because she is second in command. And all respect is due, likewise, to this delightful creature," indicating the gray monkey, "Chimène, who is third in command. You will find this animal as sweet as she is intelligent—I speak of the monkey—and she is so sensitive that . . ."

At this moment something took place which was to have serious consequences. Whilst Gaud, unmindful of the leader's speech, examined the jeweled clasps of her scarlet gloves, the monkey, fascinated by Guillette's curly hair, seized a ringlet and gave a sharp tug. As Guillette struck out blindly at the monkey, Gaud lifted her switch, and brought it down sharply across the face of the girl. Guillette lowered her head to hide the quick, involuntary tears.

Then Gaud went back to examining her jewels, a mocking smile curving her lips. Swaying with pain, Guillette did not utter a sound, but she fastened her clear eyes upon Gaud's cold hard ones, and the two remained thus for a moment.

"That's a good lesson for you," Buron smiled. "All the same, it's too bad to have marred that pretty face. Send the girl to me this evening at the Monastery, and I'll try to comfort her. And just so that no one will pick a quarrel with her meantime, I'll station a guard in front of the door, because as you know better than I, Father, the flesh is weak, and my soldiers have never yet been able to resist a pretty face. Goodby; I trust we shall meet again. Oh, I almost forgot— the purpose of this little visit: please inform all the peasants that I am taking up residence on their hospitable island. They may rent their land for five sols each hearth, and it just may be that there will be a few little duties—oh, but we can talk about those later. At the first move of a peasant against one of my men, you will naturally be hanged from the highest branch of that oak over there. Meanwhile, give me your blessing, Father—because I think I'm going to need it!"

And without another word, he wheeled his horse about, spurred it, and rode away at a canter, followed by Gaud and two of the horsemen, whilst the third dismounted near the door and attached his bridle to a bronze ring fastened in the wall for the purpose.

~ VI ~

BROTHER AUGUSTIN had been watching from a little distance away, and as soon as Buron had gone, he ran to Father Samson, who was bathing Guillette's wound.

"Still more Bretons are here," he cried. "You can see them already climbing the cliffs. They're on foot, and they have dogs with them."

Father Samson signaled to Guillette and the friar and they followed him along the ruined choir, overgrown with lichen, under half-crumbled arches which had been part of the old refectory, through bushes which hid a portion of the wall, to an old bronze door. He chose a key from the chain at his waist, inserted it in the lock, and, very slowly and carefully, pushed open the door inch by inch on its creaking hinges.

The three fugitives went silently down the steps which it had hidden, and as Guillette and Brother Augustin closed it behind them, the priest seized a resin torch from a secret niche, lit it, and led the way down the dark vaulted passageway. The flickering light made fantastic shadows on the walls, until the mysterious path seemed full of strange and menacing shapes, lurking in every age-yellowed nook and cranny. Half-vanished inscriptions on the walls caught and held the uncertain light, whilst all around the three the un-fathomable shadows were heavy with the silence of years.

"We are in the catacombs of the Monastery," explained the priest in a whisper which echoed back and forth down the narrow passageway, "and directly above is the old cemetery. The monks were so afraid that the mortal remains of their brothers would be molested that they brought them down here in secret, every year, on All Saints' Eve."

Suddenly to Guillette the place was full of the spirits of that ancient day, and her terrified ears caught what seemed an echo of their voices, through a thin, almost forgotten organ chant, a dirge for these same dead.

All at once she saw Father Samson place his foot

on the first rung of a rusted ladder, and she watched, fascinated, as he pulled himself high enough to reach a trap-door in the roof. She followed the two priests up into a sort of tiny cell, and climbed over its sides as they did. Then she realized that they had just stepped out of a sort of empty, uncovered sarcophagus, in the center of a great vaulted crypt. All about her were other sarcophagi, arranged like the points of a giant star; atop each one a black porphyry monk lay asleep, stone hands crossed piously on stone breast, stone eyelids closed over unseeing stone eyes.

"This is the Sanctuary crypt," said Father Samson. "And these are the tombs of the Monastery priors, from St. Magloire's time until the pillaging of his relics. Perhaps it was those Breton thieves who made the passageway! At any rate, no one knows anything about it. You must swear, Guillette, as I have, never to tell any one about it unless it is a matter of life and death. . . ."

The sun shone upon the upper steps of a stairway at the back of the crypt, and when the three had gone down them through the church in back of the altar, they found themselves outside in the fullness of the golden morning light.

The old man touched Guillette's shoulder. "You

must run to Lucas, my child. Perhaps he can find a way to leave the Island. I shall pray to the Saint for you both. As for you, Augustin, you must sound the alarm."

And pausing for a moment, head bowed and hands clasped, he whispered, "Holy Saint, intercede with God for these two children. They are under your special protection. Were they not to have been married on your feast-day?"

As Guillette set off towards Little Sark, the air was suddenly filled with the portentous voice of the bells. "Buron, Bu-ron," they seemed to say, until a vast whispered chorus took up the menacing words, "Buron approaches, Buron has come back." And all over the Island, fishermen and farmers at work heard the doleful refrain, and dropping plows in the midst of the furrows or nets heavy with fish, they ran with their wives and children in search of safety, those who owned boats to the sea, those less blessed with worldly goods to the hidden and almost undiscoverable caves at the base of the Island, which had served so often before as places of protection and refuge.

⤳ VII ⤳

Across the Island, pursued by the doleful bells. Over the Coupée to Little Sark. Guillette's heart seemed ready to burst from her body as she heard the bells impelling her forward, and when suddenly they were cut off in mid-note, it seemed to her that the silence, unbroken save by the frightened cries of Island gulls, was more agonizing than the insistent din which had sounded only a moment before. Doubtless Brother Augustin had paid with his life for his warning to the Island folk. All at once, another grimmer sound rent the sparkling air, a gunshot somewhere in the distance, its echoes lost amid the human cries which followed it. Looking back, Guillette saw that her house was not the only one to be burned; other smudges of smoke were dark against the blue sky, and she thought,

35

with a sob, of her family and those from the other
flaming cottages.

She had now reached the Coupée and was half-way
across the narrow path, over heights below which the
white-capped waves pounded furiously, when she
paused quickly. A few steps ahead of her Buron,
Gaud, and their escorts, hidden until now by a protruding bit of land, had just dismounted and were
trying to persuade their terrified horses, hoof after
timorous hoof, across the dizzying path. Buron wished
to turn back, Guillette gathered from her vantage
point, well hidden behind the yellow blossoms of a
clump of gorse, and Gaud screeched at him in an
anger not untinged with fear.

Guillette's heart, which had leaped into her throat
at the unexpected near-encounter, and pounded there
now until its sound seemed to fill her ears, began to
beat still more fiercely as a sound behind her—the baying of wolfhounds, hoarse masculine oaths—made her
turn her head suddenly. Already she had been sighted
by approaching foot-soldiers at the entrance of the
Coupée, and now they began to loose their dogs,
cheering them towards her. Only an instant and the
bloodthirsty beasts would be at her throat!

There was only one possible way for her to escape.

The entrance of the Coupée
By J. M. W. TURNER

She shuddered as she thought of the perilous climb down the treacherously slippery rocks at her feet. Could she ever reach in safety the large flat rock she could glimpse below? The dogs could certainly never follow her there, but even for her, born and bred on the Island, daily climber of rocks almost as dangerous as these, the steep, uncertain descent meant little less than suicide. And still Guillette attempted it—and succeeded. Young and supple as she was, she slid from ledge to slippery ledge, holding fast with her hands where searching bare feet could find no hold, clutching at sturdy bushes which grew in crannies of the otherwise barren rocks, until at last, throwing herself flat on the rock at the bottom, she realized that, for the moment at least, she was safe. Only now, as she looked up at the heights from which she had come, did her eyes, wide with the terror she had had no time to feel, fill with tears.

Meanwhile, the soldiers on the Coupée above had watched with amazed amusement the obviously hopeless struggles of the girl. One or two had pointed their arquebuses at her, though the distance was too great for accurate aim, while the others had contented themselves with dislodging stones and rolling them downhill towards each precarious haven afforded by the rocks. Then Gaud, who had been watching the sport, spied a goat-trail winding down the cliff; calling to one of the men, she bade him follow the path to a point just above the flat rock where Guillette crouched. He obeyed her orders, and when he had reached the place she had indicated, he set fire to the brush and stood back to admire the scarlet tongues of flame which licked down the cliff, until it seemed certain that Guillette must be burned or smothered, surrounded as she was by the invading fire.

Guillette realized now that nothing short of a miracle could save her. Her envious eyes followed a sure-footed rabbit as he fled the encroaching heat; the hum of a bumblebee feasting upon a flower caught her ear. All at once, a gust of wind blew sharp, stinging smoke nearer the flower where the bee rested; spreading his wings he rose up, up—and flew out of sight.

Then Guillette knew what she herself must do. If the bee had flown, so would she. She stood up, walked with unhesitating steps as near as possible to the edge of the rock, caught a deep breath, and dove head first into space. The spreading smoke hid her from her enemies, and the slant of the cliff prevented them from seeing her dive into the sea, swirling and roaring thirty feet below.

ᵛᵛᵛ VIII ᵛᵛᵛ

FORTUNATELY the waters of the pool were deep enough to allow Guillette, an expert diver, to turn and come to the surface without being dashed against the sharp rocks. Now she swam the brief distance to a small stretch of sand at the cliff's base, and shivering as she was in her soaking clothes, she managed to climb out, safe from sight of the Bretons on the ledge above.

A little while later she reached Lucas' house, vine-covered and scarlet with flowers. Here Lucas' sisters were already at work, wrapping some food and clothing in a piece of homespun cloth.

"The Bretons have reached the Coupée," she told them. "We must leave right away."

Lucas, who had been sitting on a stool, raised a

miserable face from his hands. "My boat is gone," he said. "Only a little while ago, at the first sound of the bells, a neighbor from the Vacquerie begged to use it to save the women and children, and the old people. God knows I didn't want to go without you or Coryse and Douce-Marie—what was there to do but let him have it? Look—you can see them down there, drawing out to sea. Heaven knows how far they'll be able to go in that overloaded little boat."

"What is to become of us?"

"Surely the Guernsey folk must have seen the smoke by now," whispered Corisande, her flower-petal lips trembling, her blue eyes clouded with tears, as she brushed away a heavy golden curl. "Anyway, when the Sark people reach there, they'll warn them. Help will certainly come by to-morrow."

"But we haven't time even to reach the caves," protested Guillette. "The Bretons are upon us. Listen! You can hear their hounds baying. . . ."

"I've always heard that the pit in back of our house was the entrance to one of the old silver mines," said Douce-Marie, the youngest. "Why couldn't we hide ourselves there?"

Guillette smiled in spite of herself at the tender, childlike face, fresh-cheeked and gentle.

A cottage in Little Sark

But Lucas had already picked up a horn lantern, lit the candle it held, and, followed by the three girls, was even now leading the way to the entrance, barely visible behind the rocks. The way down the steep incline was a perilous one, for the shaft had fallen into sad disrepair since the days of the Romans who had built it. In places the fetid water reached to the fugitives' knees, and they had to crawl with hands held out before their faces to escape the bats' nests along the roof of the passage. Nevertheless they pressed on and on, with a feeling of security which grew with every step they took away from the passage's entrance. From time to time they came to widenings in the passage, and here, they imagined, the unhappy prisoners and slaves of the long-dead days had been forced to work, digging the precious metal from earthen walls. The four of them could hear, in their minds' ear, the swish of whips falling upon sweat-shining backs of luckless workers who had fallen behind.

Corisande shuddered, and gave tongue to the thought that oppressed them all. "How they must have suffered," she murmured, her own soft heart heavy with pity.

The principal gallery sloped gently; but from time to time another, narrower corridor opened off to left or right, a corridor whose sharper incline made it apparent that its end lay below the surface of the sea. It was a terrifying thought to the four—that they might lose themselves in this maddening maze, with, for companions, only the bright-eyed rats who fled forward now at their approach.

In places the path became so strait that they had to press against its damp sides to progress at all; meanwhile, in back of them they could hear a low rumbling which told them that the way they had come was cut off by crumbling walls, and that now no way remained for them save forward. At the thought that they might all be buried alive forever in this rat-infested sepulcher, Lucas dug still more furiously, his hands clawing at the moist earth like those of a creature possessed, trying to open up a further way. He paused for a moment with the sickening conviction that they were in the wrong passage, that they had lost their road and would now never reach the foot of the cliff.

Suddenly, the darkness was pierced by a thin ray of light at the end of the corridor, a ray of daylight towards which they traveled with new hope, until, through the hole which had admitted it, they could glimpse a patch of blue sky and smell once more the freshness of the outside air, salty and delicious. Looking about them, they discovered that they were on a tiny platform of stones, used long ago for the shipping of minerals, but since abandoned. Across from them they glimpsed the tiny isle of the Étacq. This was a deserted portion of the coast-line, and since, surely, the Bretons would never think of searching here, they decided to pass the rest of the day and the night at the mine's entrance, rather than attempt the perilous return to the house at Fontaine Bay.

⛧ IX ⛧

Two horsemen drew rein before the open doors of a group of deserted houses. One of them, putting down his blue pennant, took a piece of vellum from his sleeve and began to unfold it, whilst the other lifted his blue-bannered trumpet to his lips and, tipping it skyward, played over and over a four-noted melody. Then the herald read his proclamation, in a voice clouded by a thick Breton accent:

"Hear, hear, O folk of Sark:

"After to-morrow noon, every deserted house will be burned to the ground. You are forbidden, under pain of death, to attempt to leave the island or to hide in the caves; all fugitives who are discovered will be cast into the sea if they are men, given over to the soldiers for their pleasure, if women, and thrown into the pigsties if children. All arms and weapons are to be given up to the Armorers who are commissioned to receive them.

"Every man of working age must present himself each morning at dawn at the Monastery, to labor on the fortifications.

"Half your provisions, meat or harvest, must be handed over for the sustenance of the army of occupation.

"Girls and women will be respected, unless they offer needless or humiliating refusals to the soldiers.

"Captain Buron, Lord of Bruel and Marquis of Rosporden, promises his protection to all those who conform to his orders. He is pleased to think that with coöperation the mutual relations of soldiers and inhabitants will continue friendly."

Again a sharp blast upon the trumpet; then the herald folded the manuscript and rode away at a trot, followed by his companion.

And while, in the caves below, the owners of the deserted houses crouched hungry and frightened, the soldiers who had taken possession of the houses began to make merry, laughing and drinking, singing songs of their own prowess and cunning. But Buron's news was soon to spread over the whole Island, for a little boy who had been hiding during the herald's reading of his proclamation set out in haste for the caves, whither the Sark folk had fled with what provisions they could muster, the women carrying their babies while the men led as many of the cattle as could be persuaded from their grazing grounds. They all heard the child's news in a fever of indecision; the men, mindful of the falsity of Buron's promises, loath to put themselves in his power by going back to their homes, the women, already cold and hungry, eager to seize on any hope, however slight.

"We can't stay here much longer," they pleaded. "We haven't any food, nor enough water! It's so damp here that the children and the calves are already beginning to cough. If we must die, let us at least die in the sunlight!"

And at last they won over their men. Then the weary trudge began, their shoulders burdened with their poor provisions, their skinny beasts driven before them, up the cliffs and back to their homes, many of them already no more than charred beams and gray ashes, rising and falling in the sun-heavy breeze.

ᛯ X ᛯ

NEXT morning, after a sleep blurred with night-
mares, Lucas decided with the approval of the
girls to go home by way of the cliff, not only to bring
back supplies which they sadly needed, but to hear
the latest news of the invaders as well.

The word of Buron's proclamation, which he heard
from every side, made him decide that he must follow
the line of least resistance—go to the Monastery every
dawn to do his required service, to save his house
from the flames. Every night he would come back to
the girls and take care of them during the long hours
of darkness here in the refuge which he forbade them
to leave at any time during the day.

Thus it was that the next day's sunrise found him
hard at work, side by side with the other Islanders,

47

upon a defense wall which was being built under the supervision of surly soldiers who watched the proceedings with sneering smiles and now and again a harshly menacing order when one of the laborers paused for a moment to straighten his bare back, or gaze for an instant out to sea.

Only during the brief rest periods were the workers allowed to speak to one another; when the signal for the tiny relaxation came, they all threw themselves full length upon the ground and began to whisper discouragedly, too tired and too conscious of the danger to form more than scant phrases with their dry, sun-cracked lips.

"When the Bretons landed down at our place," said a Longuepointe fisherman, "some of the men tried to fight them. The Bretons killed them—every last one. Some tried to hide in the caves, and wouldn't come out, but the Bretons had an answer to that, too. They lighted a fire at the cave mouth and smoked 'em —just like hams. The rest were drowned." Even told as it was in a tired, matter-of-fact voice, the story sent an odd chill down the back of every listener.

Then some one else broke the silence. "Speaking of fire," he said, "have you seen the great fire they light every night up on the hill, and the lanterns they stick

Gouliot Cave

on the cows' horns? Do you know why they do it? It's
to make sailors think they're the lights of St. Pierre
Port! How can the Governor of Guernsey let them go
on? Why doesn't he send boats over to save us? Isn't
it terrible?"

They nodded their heads and clicked their tongues.
An old farmer from the other side of the Island spoke
at last, in a trembling voice. "Buron's looking all over
for little Guillette. She's run away from him twice,
and he's sworn to catch her for himself. He's having
a great party Sunday, at the Monastery—every girl on
the Island will have to be there, or she'll be caught
and sold at auction to the Bretons. Imagine! She'll
have to stand up in the market, all naked . . ."

"Some people say they're going to put us back to
work in the silver mines. . . ."

As always, Lucas had brought along his mandore,
and sitting a little apart from the others, he played
softly on its strings, making the music tell of the bit-
ter pain in his heart, taking the place of words he
could not utter. But the name of Guillette caught his
ear, and the mention of the silver mines caused him
to pluck one of the strings with such force that it
snapped.

"How too bad," whispered a voice behind him.

Turning, his eyes met the hard blue ones of Gaud, who smiled back at him imperiously, thrusting forward a tiny foot in an embroidered shoe from under the full skirt of her low-bodiced brocade gown.

Behind her stood her attendant, scarcely less elegant or less lovely than she, in her velvet and taffeta dress, betraying her less important position only by the fact that it was she who bore the little gray monkey in her arms, and she who led the curly-haired white spaniel by a leash from its gold and silver collar.

"Look at this lad, Rosario," said Gaud, with an admiring chuckle, as she studied him from under heavy painted lids. "Isn't he handsome? Play some more, friend—your music delights me, enchants me——"

And the two young women stood and gazed at Lucas. Just then, the work signal was given, and Lucas took up his spade instead of his mandore. His companions, as if in answer to Gaud's command, began to sing the words of a plaintive air, but Lucas, disturbed by what the workman had said of Guillette, remained silent. Gaud turned towards him, pivoting carefully on her high heels, and, looking up into his face with her insolent eyes, went on talking to him as if there had been no interruption.

"What's your name?" she asked, a mocking smile curling her lips. "Who taught you to play so beautifully?"

Lucas stopped digging, leaned on his spade, and stared from one to the other of the two women. Then, with a shrug of his broad shoulders, he set to work once more, tossing a clod of earth in their direction as though for answer.

Gaud blushed at the insult, her face reddening as if she had been slapped across the cheek. None the less, she repeated her question, with no better luck this time than before. The man working at Lucas' side answered, fearful that Lucas might be severely punished as an example.

"His name is Lucas, Princess, but we call him the Minstrel, because he's so skilful on the mandore. But he's not much of a talker; you must realize that he isn't used to addressing anybody of your rank. For every two words he spoke, he'd make three mistakes."

"Is he married?"

"Not yet, Ladyship, but he's just about to be—to the prettiest little girl on the whole Island—and sharper than you and me put together!—even if she has annoyed your Lord Marquis of Rosporden—the old gray Owl, as we call him!"

"She wouldn't be, by any chance, the little wench that I had to correct the other day because she was disrespectful to my monkey?"

Lucas had just dug his spade into the ground, and at these words he brought it up quickly, laden with dark brown earth. But instead of depositing the load in front of him, he raised it suddenly and flung it, with all his strength, into the face of the young woman, wreaking havoc to her dainty hat, her thin blouse.

Furious, Gaud signaled to her two soldiers to seize Lucas, and within a moment he had fallen powerless to the ground.

"Take him to the Monastery," she ordered, her voice thick with anger; then, as the men started to drag him away, "Take along the mandore, too."

She walked away, swaying from her green velvet-clad hips, followed by Rosario, who still carried the little monkey, Chimène, and by the curly spaniel.

As they drew away, the peasants, who had paused for a moment to watch the little scene, went back to their work, this time silently, with no song to break the dull thud of spade against earth. The old man who had spoken to Gaud scratched his ear.

"I guess I was wrong to say what I did," he muttered. "But I was just trying to avoid exactly what did happen. What could I have said that wouldn't have made her so mad?"

And he looked around at the lowered heads, and continued to scratch his ear.

ᥭᥴ XI ᥴᥭ

THE sea stretched out to the horizon line, smooth and unbroken where its blue waves turned to gray; choppy and white-foamed here at the feet of the three girls who sat all morning watching its ebb and flow from the rocky shore of their well-hidden refuge. Each of the three thought to hide her own fears from the others, and they chattered gaily, with only the dark waters of doubt behind their eyes to tell one another that fear surrounded them. Towards the middle of the afternoon, when the suspense grew unbearable, they decided to bathe in the little natural pool not far from their retreat, the Pool of Venus it was called because of its incredibly clear water, through which might be seen bright-hued algæs clinging to rocky bottom and sides.

The girls slipped off their clothes, and stood for a moment stretching up their arms to the warm rays of the sun. Then, laughing as they forgot their worries for this moment, they dived into the sparkling water, splashing and kicking with delight as the ripples they made in the pool lapped against their straight young bodies, washing away their fears of the past days.

Suddenly they heard an alien sound. The barking of dogs at the exit of the mine startled them into silence; then, terrified, they watched as three men followed the dogs from the cave. The men surveyed the scene with leering smiles, and only the glistening slippery rocks saved the girls from their immediate onslaught. Forgetting their clothes, everything, except the panic which overtook them, the girls pulled out towards the near-by sea, with the long, practised strokes of experienced swimmers, not wasting breath in words. The Bretons raced after them to the edge of the rocks, then, impotent with rage, they had to content themselves with throwing pebbles and insults after them.

Guillette, a stronger swimmer than the other two, soon drew out of the Bretons' range, and indeed the Bretons had difficulty in seeing her brown head, so similar in color to the dark rocks between which she darted. But the two sisters, more easily out of breath, had to pause to rest on a sand-bar, and their golden heads, gleaming like coins in the sunlight, marked them out easily to their pursuers.

Guillette tried to turn and come back to them, but she saw soon enough that her efforts were wasted, for she was caught in an irresistible current. There was nothing for it but to abandon her companions, and allow herself to be carried by the sweeping waters down to the Étacq. Clutching at the seaweed, she climbed ashore to a cleft in the steep side, where, stretched out between two rocks, she gave herself up for a moment to the blessed, refreshing rays of the sun, so delicious on her tired, panting body.

When she was rested enough, she decided to explore the tiny island, and, clambering over sharp-pointed rocks, she set out for its summit. She stooped for a cooling drink at a thin stream of fresh water, bordered by ferns and mosses, and went on up the slope. From the top of the hill, she could see the bay stretching out before her, and the cliffs of the island facing her were black near the water where the foam made an edging of lace, dark yellow on their steep slopes, and at their tops, rich green with the spring foliage of trees. The girl knew that the current which

The great rocks at Little Sark

had borne her here would carry her further, to the great rock on one side of Little Sark, and when she had made a thorough tour of the island, even to the caves, half filled now with the waters of the rising tide, she slipped back into the sea, and felt herself carried effortlessly away to the coast of Sark, to a spot not far from a little cut in the overhanging cliffs. Climbing ashore, she found her way through the giant rhubarb plants which lined a trickling brook to a cottage, whose chimney, well protected against witches by the traditional perch for them alongside it, breathed forth a stream of blue smoke.

It was only then that Guillette realized that she was stark naked.

Hastily plucking a few of the big rhubarb leaves, she fashioned herself a wide belt, and she must have liked her reflection in the pond's waters as she bent over them, for she smiled fleetingly at her own image there.

She stepped up to the house, and in answer to her sharp rapping a gray head, almost covered with a black sunbonnet, appeared at the window and inquired her business.

"Open the door, Grandmother. It's Guillette, Gilles's daughter, from the Éperquerie. I need your help."

"Great heavens! Guillette! What on earth are you doing here, all naked under those leaves?"

"Please, Grandmother, that's just why I've come to see you. Have you any clothes I could borrow? . . . So you stayed, too, did you, Grandmother?"

"Well, for goodness' sakes, what would they want with an old woman like me? It's the young girls like you who are in danger," she said, as she opened the door. "My boy stayed, too—he's just come back from his duty, and he's all worn out, poor lad. He's asleep. I could lend you his smock and his Sunday trousers. Won't you have a glass of cider and a piece of bread, too? Have you had anything to eat since morning?" And clicking her tongue and shaking her head, the old woman began to help the girl to pull on the boy's clumsy clothes. Then Guillette must needs sit down and eat a bite, for the woman would not hear of her going away hungry.

"And Lucas?" she said suddenly to the girl. "Do you know that that wicked Gaud had him shut up in the Monastery this noon?"

Guillette jumped to her feet.

"Lucas? At the Monastery? Are you sure? Gaud had Lucas taken prisoner?"

"My boy was working right beside him, and he says

that Lucas threw a clod of dirt at Gaud's nose, because she was saying evil things about you."

Guillette seized the cake knife from the table.

"Please lend me this little knife, Grandmother. And
thank you for everything. I'll never forget what you've
done. Good-by—I have things to do—and they can't
wait."

And with a rebellious toss of her bright head, Guillette set out at a run to attempt to rescue Lucas.

ᔒ XII ᔓ

A N OLD cell of the Monastery had been trans-
formed into a pleasant room, and in the light
of a crystal lantern hung from its ceiling Gaud and
Rosario were deep in conversation.

Seated before her mirror, Gaud studied her own
reflection with interest and approval. The snowy
whiteness of her arms and throat stood out sharply
against her low-cut brown silk robe, and the heavy
golden curls which Rosario was even now arranging
were full of warm lights. In the mirror she watched
the Spanish girl's deft fingers, as they made a smooth
part precisely in the center of her head, and fastened
her hair again in the winged olive-green head-dress
which came down in a point on her fair, broad forehead.

All the while, Chimène, the little gray monkey, perched opposite the two women, watched them closely, aping in the small looking-glass in his hand the very tilt of Gaud's head, her expression of satisfaction with her own beauty, the instinctive little pat she gave to her hair when Rosario had finished dressing it, before she began to bathe Gaud's arms and face in the delicately scented water. He studied carefully the girl's swift movements as she applied first a smooth lotion, then, dipping her fingers into a small jar on the dressing-table, outlined Gaud's full lips with pink, then carefully traced the haughty eyebrows with a charcoal stick.

Gaud rose, slipped off her chemise, and covered herself with a rich, silver-trimmed skirt, a tight blue bodice, a very thin tucked blouse.

"Let me have just a little more white powder on my forehead—yes, and a touch more pink on my cheeks," ordered Gaud, "and hand me my pendant of jade, my talisman."

Rosario obeyed. "I don't believe there is any one half so elegant as Madame in the whole English court," she whispered. "That little eel-fisherman is going to be overcome."

"Be still, Rosario. You mustn't talk like that about

my Lucas. You're only an ignorant child—you couldn't possibly understand how thrilled I was by his music this morning. It filled me with a delicious trembling. And, oh! how his eyes flamed when I made him so angry. He was like a young cock, so full of life and fury. Whatever he is, he pleases me tremendously. By the way, you've surely told the Owl that I'm a little indisposed, and won't be able to dine with him this evening? How did he take that?"

"Very well indeed, Madame. He asked me to come down and keep him company, after I had put you to bed, and to be sure to bring my tambourine," Rosario answered, as she fastened a heavy enamel and turquoise necklace about Gaud's throat.

"Is that so! That Owl! Won't you have a good time, though, poor little Rosario! So the two blondes that he brought back from the hunt to-day aren't enough. Or maybe the soldiers had ruined them. All the same, I thought the little one they call Douce-Marie very fresh and pretty, and even the big one, Corisande, won't be bad when her face has healed."

"Perhaps Madame is right," replied Rosario, kneeling to pull on Gaud's silken hose and slippers, "but it's all right, if he's looked at them. He's given orders to have their faces treated with oil, and to have them

rubbed with Holland balm, so that they'll be present-
able for the festival on Sunday. I have a sort of idea
that he would have preferred the third—the one
who's always escaping him, the one he talks about all
the time."

"You didn't forget what I bade you do about the
boat?"

"The Owl's personal boat is ashore, as always, up
by the cave where Lucas is imprisoned. I put everything in the chest behind it—guinea-hen aspic, crack-
nels, wine, two crystal goblets. You'll find there a
watch-light, too, and candles and tinderbox. The key
to the cave is hanging on your key-ring, next to the
key which opens the lock of Lucas' chain."

Rosario slipped a large earth-colored cloak around
her mistress' shoulders, and handed her a nose-mask
of black velvet. Gaud took the crystal ball of it between her teeth, and smiled with satisfaction as she
saw that the mask hid her face except for her eyes
and her chin.

"That's all right," she said, slipping it off. "You
seem to have thought of everything. Be careful, and
if the Owl should happen to wish to see me in my
room this evening, you manage to get here ahead of
him. Then you can imitate my voice, and refuse to

let him in. I expect to be back to-morrow at dawn."

As she opened the door out on to the gallery, the full brilliance of the moon in the dark night burst upon her, and she made her way through a hidden passage down to the cliff in a light as bright as day. With a leap Chimène followed after in her footsteps.

When she was sure that her mistress was safely out of sight, Rosario sat down in the chair which Gaud had just left, took her mirror, and studied her own beautiful face with considerable pleasure. Then she dipped into the pots and jars of ointments and paints spread before her, giving herself up to the care she owed to her own delicious loveliness.

ᔰ XIII ᔰ

THE light of candles in the huge onyx candelabras
flickered through the civet-scented room as Rosario's tambourine made music for the quick steps of her
dance. One arm waved the gossamer scarf with which
she wove graceful patterns; her sun-browned legs
flashed in and out under the skirt of her light tunic
as she followed the complicated, sensuous movements
of the bolero. Watching her from his deep arm-chair,
Buron's one eye glittered in his evil face, and from
time to time his brocade-sleeved arm moved out to
grasp a sweetmeat from the jeweled bonbonnière
beside him.

Rosario whirled and bent before him, her lips
parted in a smile of pleasure as her body sank to the
floor, only her small firm breasts, straining from their

silver casing, raised as if she offered them to the man who watched. Between the beats of the tambourine there was no sound save the clinking of her thin bracelets.

Little by little the rhythm grew swifter; she threw away her scarf and her tambourine, seized off her tunic and swayed before him in a cambric shift, through which he could see the undulating smooth roll of her hips. Catching the castanets attached to her wrists in her palms, she began to accompany her movements with their incessant clicking, turning, gyrating, whirling, while her heavy-lidded eyes, with their passionate invitation, never left those of Buron, who remained motionless in his chair. Her movements grew more and more abandoned, until at last, with a violent leap and a guttural cry, she threw herself, panting, at the knees of the half-blind old villain, bending her brown head as if submitting in advance to his desires. The scent of her moist skin disturbed Buron, and, lowering his face to hers, he took her two hands in his own.

Just at this instant, some one knocked at the door, and as it swung wide Guillette came in, smiling, as though she had forgotten her just-past fears, looking very determined in her little boy's trousers.

Buron was so astonished that he forgot to push away the Spaniard who pressed against him.

"You, here? Who brought you?"

"Nobody brought me, my lord. Didn't you offer yourself, when I saw you at the Monastery, to take me under your protection? I've come to recall your promise to you. Here I am."

"You came here all by yourself, of your own free will? What do you mean?"

He studied her closely, from her bare feet, her delicate thighs, to the curly hair cut short like a boy's. Was she laughing at him? One look at her clear eyes, her guileless smile, convinced him that she was not.

"I thought that you liked me a little."

"But of course I do, child. I like you a great deal. With a—ahum—with a fervent liking," he added, looking at the young figure beneath the fisherman's tunic. "But why did you come to me?"

Guillette looked at him for a moment, then with a yielding movement of her body, she lowered her eyes.

"Come and sit here by me," said Buron, surprised in spite of himself. "What can I do to make you like me? Ask for whatever you want—I grant it to you in advance. And while we're waiting, perhaps you'd like a glass of wine?"

"Sire, I want you to release my two friends, Corisande and Douce-Marie. I want to take their place with you. I want to be the only one to serve you. Oh, you'll see how lovingly I'll care for you."

Buron looked at her again, seeing her fresh pink lips parted to show her even white teeth, and, because he wished nothing more than to believe her, was soon convinced.

"I promise you that it shall be done. And then? Surely there is something else you wish?"

"Something else? Oh, Sire, you have done too much already. What more could I ask? And yet there is something . . . I'm not fit to stand before you in these clothes that I had to borrow because I lost mine when that band of ruffians interrupted our swim today. Would it be possible for you to let me have some others? Surely Princess Gaud has some old gown that would be more fitting for me to wear when I come to do you honor?"

Buron took her face between his two hands and kissed her forehead.

"You are very lovely as you are. But you would be more beautiful still in one of Gaud's dresses. Rosario will take you to her dressing-room, and you may choose whatever you like. Then, when you are satisfied with your clothes, come back to me, for your service begins this very evening. We'll have supper together. Rosario, show her the way, and bring her back as soon as you can. Meanwhile, I shall see that your friends are set free, and shall order a supper good enough for such a charming young lady."

He rose with difficulty—for at the time he had lost his eye, he had received a leg wound which made him limp painfully. He leaned upon his swordstick, elegantly devised in the shape of a beautiful cane, and walked politely to the door with the two girls. At his command the guard in the hall hurried off to free Corisande and Douce-Marie.

Kneeling at Buron's feet, Rosario had taken in every detail of the scene played before her, and she had watched now the Marquis, now Guillette, with an enigmatic smile. When Buron stood up, she took a candelabra, and without a word led the girl into the passageway to Gaud's apartments, not far off. She had no more than closed the door and set down her light when she felt a small strong hand clasped over her mouth, and the blade of a knife pressing the warm perfumed flesh just over her heart.

"If you scream, I'll push the knife in, so that it really hurts," said Guillette's calm voice.

"That's useless," answered Rosario. "I want nothing better than to help you. You want to know where Gaud is? I'll tell you, if you'll only drop that knife. Suppose you should wound me."

Guillette's hand had dropped from the Spaniard's mouth, and she drew the knife a little away.

"Why isn't she here? And where is Lucas?"

Rosario turned her deep-colored eyes towards the young girl and shrugged her shoulders.

"Why isn't Gaud here? Because she went to meet Lucas, who is shut up in the Cave of the Boutiques. If you hurry, you'll be able to get there as soon as she does. Then if ever will be the time to use your knife. But you'll have to hurry. If you get rid of her, Buron will give me her place, and that will suit me much better than being her handmaiden. But before you go, you'd better tie me to the bed, as soon as I've fixed this gag. And good luck! Go out by the small door at your right."

As she spoke, Rosario had been pulling whatever scarves and laces she could find out of the chest, and now, fitting a gag into place, she held out her hands and feet to Guillette, who tied her securely to a chair before she left the room in search of Gaud.

ᔥ XIV ᔥ

THE twelve-pound weight on Lucas' chain pulled
heavily as he walked back and forth in his iron-
barred prison in the Cave of the Boutiques. From time
to time he paused his melancholy thoughts to look
out through the bars, as if he might discover in the
world outside some solution to his hopeless problems.
As for himself, he neither wished nor hoped for anything save a speedy death; but what was to become of
his betrothed and his sisters, what outrages might they
not already have suffered at Buron's hands? For the
first time, he was so discouraged that he could not
bring himself to pick up his mandore thrown on the
ground beside him. Worn out at last with his weary
thoughts, he lay down on his back, his eyes, unseeing,
fastened upon the vaulted ceiling of the grotto.

Outside, the world was black with night, save for a narrow strip of moonlight through a crack in the rocks over his head, sign that out on the windswept cliffs the moon was shining.

Suddenly a tiny noise caught his attention. Some one had opened the door of his prison, then closed it carefully. In the rays of the lamp it carried, he could barely make out a masked figure wrapped in a cloak, coming towards him. A monkey perched upon its shoulder.

"Well, Lucas, are you going to be stingy with your words again, my friend?"

Gaud put down her lantern on a protruding ledge, and throwing back her cloak, held her lovely bare arms out to him. She took his head in her heavily ringed hands, and began to stroke his hair gently.

"Didn't you understand, Lucas, that you—please me? Why are you so different from other men? No one else would have been able to resist so long. Would you ever have dreamed that you could make me feel like this?"

Lucas shook his head, indifferent. Gaud went on, in her cajoling voice, "You have disturbed me since the first time I saw you, since the first time I heard you play your mandore. You made me dream of a world I never guessed; don't you want to take me there with you? A boat is waiting for us, just outside. It's a warm, calm night, Lucas; the sky is very clear. The sea is silver; my oars will make only faint ripples in it as I row you, quietly, so that I can hear you sing your love-song. I have had many lovers, Lucas, but I have never had a sweetheart. Will you be my sweetheart?"

She dropped her cloak and sat down beside him, leaning her face towards his that he might catch the faint fragrance of her perfumed hair. But Lucas did not move, nor did he say anything. It was as if he had not heard her words at all. She put her arm around his neck, and whispered softly into his ear.

"Think, my Lucas, that my power here is limitless. Buron, who likes to be called the Destroyer, is a coward. He trembles before those he commands. If I wished, I could make you the leader of the Bretons to-morrow. His spoils of war are all here, in this cave. If we took them, we should be rich forever. Only think of the écus, the doubloons, the nobles, the ducats, the sequins, the cruzades, the rixdales, in these barrels! And I know of others, full of bars of gold and silver. And those chests are running over with pearls, with topazes, with sapphires, with sardonyx and bézoards. Now it's perfectly possible that riches don't interest you. But consider, on the other hand, that if I choose I can have you torn apart by four horses. It's up to you, my love."

And still Lucas seemed not to hear. His gaze passed over Gaud's head and fastened itself on the crack in the vault of the cave. It seemed strange to him that he could no longer see the moonlight through it.

But the young woman went on in a low voice, barely opening her lips, "Listen, my darling. I'll tell you a secret. On Sunday Buron is going to have a great festival, a real marriage festival, because all the girls of Sark will have to take part, and by twilight every girl who hasn't chosen a husband among the soldiers will be put up at auction. It's going to be really delightfully funny, as you can see. A little while ago, they brought a big, blue-eyed girl from Little Sark, Corisande, her name is, and another sweet one called Douce-Marie. But the prize of the whole lot will be a girl named Guillette. You must have heard of her. Of course it's possible that Buron will save her for himself, because he is quite intrigued by her. Don't you see, Lucas, there's only one person who can stop this whim of a lustful old man: I, if I should happen to be jealous. But of course jealousy like that would certainly deserve a reward. . . ."

As she spoke, she drew still nearer to him, until her lips brushed his.

But for several moments Lucas had been watching a rope, dropping, inch by inch, through the crack in the cave's roof. It reminded him strangely of the rope Guillette used to slide down the cliff at the Éperquerie. And as soon as it touched the ground, he saw, first two slender legs, then the whole body, of Guillette, in her boy's breeches. Then, at last, he saw her rumpled head, her wide smile, her clear eyes. And just as Gaud's lips touched his, the girl slid down the rope and landed all her weight on Gaud's shoulders; as the woman turned, Guillette lashed her full in the face with the dangling rope, stinging across her features with a whistling noise.

"I owed you that from the other day, Madame. I'll spare your life now, but allow me to take my betrothed, and you can have Buron, to whom I gather you are so deeply attached. By the way, just now he's waiting at the Monastery to have supper with me. Please explain my absence to him, and beg him to excuse me. . . ."

She seized Gaud's key-ring and opened Lucas' chain,

then with his help attached it to Gaud's feet. She picked up the lantern as did Lucas his mandore, and the two of them went out the door to the boat Gaud had so thoughtfully beached near-by.

At first Chimène watched her mistress closely, imitating every gesture, but when she saw the end of the rope that had just lashed Gaud, she grabbed it in her tiny hands and climbed carefully up it to the roof.

~ XV ~

OVER the sea, white in the milky light of the moon, a little boat drew away from the coast of Sark. The whispered words of the lovers aboard mingled with the soft lapping sound of the water; sometimes the two joined their voices with the sweet notes of Lucas' mandore. And sometimes, too, they paused to stay their hunger with the food they found aboard the craft. It was not long before the cliffs of Herm showed in the distance, while those of Sark grew less and less sharp, until at last they were no more than a thin, darker line upon a dark horizon.

"Let's stop the night at Herm," Lucas said. "You'll be safe there, because the island is deserted. To-morrow evening I'll fetch my sisters, who must have

77

gone home after Buron let them free, and then all four of us can go on to Guernsey. No doubt we'll find your family there."

The barque slid softly up on a beach of powdered shells, and the two young people looked over the island from a sheltered spot beneath mosses grown tree-high. Not far from them the outlines of dolmens, clear against the sky, made them both think of the long-dead past, brought to their minds familiar stories about the strange stones.

"Those were Druid altars once," said Lucas meditatively. "People say that they offered their human sacrifices on them, before the Saint came. And witches used to come here on their broomsticks, and dance all night long. They used to fly down people's chimneys, too, and break up everything inside their houses. They drove most of the people away; the others were killed by the Bretons. That's why nobody lives here any more —only the dead, and evil spirits."

Above them, an owl uttered its mournful, questing cry, and flew off into the darkness.

"You say that nobody lives here, Lucas. But see up there, just behind the pines. Perhaps it's a star, but it looks like a little light." Guillette clung closer to his protecting arm.

And in truth a fire was glowing from the peak of a crag. They stopped to study it.

"It's not a star—yet there couldn't be anybody on the island at this time of night. Though it might be people who have fled here from Sark. Or perhaps it's a hermit, praying for the unhappy dead. Anyway, let's go on, Guillette. Whatever it is, it's living folk we'll meet."

"And what if it were the dead? Wait, look—see those great black spots in the water—they weren't there a minute ago. And hear how quiet it is—it gives me goose-flesh, it makes my blood run cold. Perhaps those spots are the sails of dead people's ships, sailing around and around the island."

"I see what you mean, Guillette—but it's only rocks that we couldn't see before because the tide was higher. It's only the current flowing past them that makes them look as if they were moving. Give me your hand, sweetheart—don't be so frightened."

"I'm not frightened when I'm with you, Lucas. But still I wouldn't care to meet spirits—especially spirits who didn't like their graves. . . ."

"We'd only have to say three Paternosters backwards, and they'd have to go away."

Behind them their shadows grew longer in the paling moonlight, and the white blooms of the furze bush seemed to be flowers of snow.

"Is it true," asked Guillette, after a pause, "that a long time ago all the people on the island changed into wild beasts at Christmastime?"

Lucas did not answer. Instead, seizing Guillette's arm, he pointed out to her, a little behind them, two spots of light, like glow-worms, or more like demon's eyes, green-tinted, staring at them intently. Another pair, further off . . . then another. They seemed to come close to Guillette and Lucas by leaps and bounds; they disappeared, only to appear again a few steps away, in another direction. Then a weird miaowing split the silence, and Lucas began to laugh.

"That time I was as frightened as you, Guillette. But those aren't devils, thank God. They're only wild cats, the descendants of the tame ones who used to live on the island when there were people here. They won't hurt us. Anyway, we're almost there. Now at last we'll see a human face. . . ."

Hidden for a moment by the great pines which crowned the summit, the light appeared again, very near now. It was a tiny watch-light, on the gable of a very low ruin of a house attached to an old windmill; no doubt the common bakehouse where the people who had lived here baked their bread from the flour ground at the mill. At the foot of the old house the ashes of a half-burned wood fire were still red, and a caldron hung above them. And crouched on the flat stone of the witches' bench sat a shape that did not seem human, hidden, but for the eagle nose, the toothless mouth, the gray-whiskered chin, under an enormous cape. It was a ragged old woman, and close by her crowded a dozen cats, their eyes glittering through the darkness. She was talking to them in her husky voice, punctuating each sentence with a scrap of meat tossed to them. "Well, my darlings, you're going to have a feast to-night. Can you guess the surprise old Sarah has for you? A lovely crow that she caught in her trap, a lovely, delicious crow. Well! Well!" she broke off suddenly, seeing the two young people, "here are some guests I didn't expect to-night."

Guillette and Lucas shivered to hear the voice that was not like a living being's voice. But Lucas stepped forward. "Good evening, Grandmother," he said uneasily. "You—you have a good heart, I'm sure."

Sarah looked up at Lucas with her wild old eyes, from under red eyelids, rose from her bench and, leaning upon her stick until she was almost bent double, hobbled up to him, to get a better look at him.

"But it's dear little Bertrand! How did you get here? What happened to you after they threw you into the sea down there? So you forgave Pascaline for marrying Sylvain when you were only three months dead? And now she's deceiving him with you! Ha— a good joke—an excellent joke. Yes, children, it's true that I have a good heart, and you shall have your share to-night. But don't forget that to-morrow it's only the cats who get fed. All the people who used to live here are cats now. After the great massacre, I came out of the cave where I was hiding, and found only dead bodies and miaowing cats. I was young then, like this little girl. But see here—this isn't Pascaline? What's your name, child, and when did you die?"

"I'm not dead at all, Grandmother. My name's Guillette, and I've just come across from Sark with Lucas, my betrothed."

Old Sarah seized her left hand. "Show me your palm, so I can see it there. . . . Oh, I greet you, Guillette of Sark, Guillette the pure! Soon you will be in great danger of death. But don't be afraid, because you will live many years, and be showered with riches and honor, thanks to the stranger who's coming into your life to-morrow. . . ."

"But Lucas, Grandmother—what about Lucas?"

"Lucas? I don't know anything about a Lucas. This lad with you is little Bertrand. He was drowned near Roches-Douvres, a long time ago."

In a near-by wood a cock crew.

"There! The night is ending. I must go back to my house—my poor old eyes would burn out in sunlight. But first I must put more tallow in my lamp. If that went out, there wouldn't be any fire on the island, and the cats wouldn't know how to make any. This is their fire, it's the Lantern of the Dead, the Watch-light of the Perished."

~ XVI ~

IN THE east the opal sky grew more and more rosy
as Lucas and Guillette, shaken by the words they
had just heard, walked away from the old woman.
Now they followed an old path, ruin-lined, to what
must once have been the market-place, as desolate
now as the path they had taken to the hilltop. Then
past the old Convent of the Cordeliers, once as
haughty and commanding as a fortress, now no more
than a heap of disordered stones like its neighbors. A
gorge in the cliff, through which they made their way,
had bit by bit been eaten away by sand and sea, until
now waves came up to break at their very feet. Suddenly a strange sound struck their ears.

"It sounds to me like a bell, and muffled voices,"
said Guillette. "Listen a minute. . . . Why, it seems

to come right up out of the sea. . . . Oh, Lucas, what is it?"

"If you hear bells, by night, upon the sea, prepare your soul for death right speedily," quoted Lucas. "I've heard that my father listened to the death warning the night before he fell from the cliffs of Vermandaye, and that he heard the bells of the submerged abbey under the water. They say that this path used to lead right across to Guernsey, and there were villages and forests where now there's only water."

They climbed to the spot where a narrow strip of water separates Herm from Jethou. Now the sun had risen from the sea, and the waves glistened and sparkled in the growing light. At this instant they glimpsed a vessel below them, pulling up anchor and gliding away.

"God be praised, Guillette," said Lucas fervently, "those bells we heard were only the tinkling of the anchor chains on the winches. And now we're at the end of our troubles, because that boat flies the cross and leopards of Normandy."

They signaled wildly to the ship, and at last must have caught the attention of the men aboard her, for a small boat was dropped into the sea and rowed back toward them. A few moments later the two young people found themselves on the quarter-deck of the boat, with the Captain and his lieutenant. Under his helmet the Captain eyed them with interest and spoke to them with courteous good-will, not untinged with surprise at this unexpected encounter.

"What were you two doing on that deserted island? You didn't see the witch, did you?"

"We escaped from Sark last evening," answered Lucas. "That poor old madwoman isn't half as frightening as Buron and Gaud."

At the name of Sark, the Captain immediately became alert and questioned Lucas closely as to the events of the last two days, his face growing grave as he listened to the story of the brutality of Buron the Destroyer and his men.

"Sark must be saved, Sire," whispered Guillette, lifting her lovely eyes to the Captain's face.

"Save Sark, child! How lightly you say it. First we'd have to find a way to land there. We're going to try, but it will be a hot battle. You'd better wait for us here. We'll come for you when we return—if we return."

"I should stay at Herm, while you go to deliver Sark? Oh, no, surely, you can't mean that. Take us along with you as pilots; nobody knows the way to the harbor better than we."

"Very well, I'll try you at least. De Glatigny, take them forward. They're going to help us miss the rocks. And now it's in God's hands."

The lieutenant signaled to them to follow him, and answered their questions as they walked.

"This is the *Belle Henriette,* out of St. Aubin on Jersey. She's armed with two eighteen-pound cannon, and four five-pound ones. Our crew is half men of Jersey, half of Guernsey, all volunteers. Several days ago we caught sight of the smoke on Sark; at night we could see the reflection of the flames reddening the sky. We hurried as fast as we could, but first we had to come to terms with the Governor of Guernsey, who didn't want to interfere. Then we had to stop here overnight, because we wanted to reach Sark by day, not daring to attempt it in the dark because of the reefs. But our Chief isn't in the habit of turning back half-way, and when he's decided something, he doesn't give up easily. He's somewhat stubborn. That's probably his only fault. His name is Sir Helier de Carteret, Seigneur of St. Ouen on the Island of Jersey."

ᔒᔓ XVII ᔖᔗ

BY ONE of those contrasts so common in the Channel Islands, the weather changed suddenly, and
the bright sunlight of early morning had turned to
heavy, cloaking mist as the *Belle Henriette* drew
near to Sark. Soon the ship herself was enmeshed in
the fog, and when the wind had fallen, the reefs were
so numerous that Sir Helier de Carteret judged it
better to lower all sails save one.

Up in the bowsprit Lucas and Guillette were pointing out the way to De Glatigny, and he in turn roared
the orders up to the helmsman, as the rocks rose, now
menacing and as high as church steeples, now mere
dots covered with sea-gulls in the white foam of the
raging waters. In order to disembark on the part of
the coast whence he could most easily take the enemy

by surprise, De Carteret had decided as soon as he reached the Island to round its northern end and attack from the south. Thus they sailed by Brecqhou. the Autelets, the Bec du Nez, the Pêcheresse, the Noire Pierre, the Grande Moie, and the Conchée, to land at last in Derrible Bay, at the foot of the Quennevez cliff.

The Captain whistled his men together on the quarter-deck. "My friends," he said to them, "we have had good luck with the weather. The fog has meant that we could reach here without being seen. The Bretons will never dream that we can climb the cliff of Derrible, it's the only side from which they're not expecting us. I myself shall take command of the port sloop, and the Jersey men shall come with me; M. de Glatigny will command the starboard sloop, with the men of Guernsey. As soon as we have landed, we will climb the slope, no matter how steep it is. After that, you will have only to follow me. Light the tinders of your arquebuses, and be very careful not to get them wet. And above all, no noise."

At these words Lucas, who had been listening to the orders with growing surprise, spoke to the Captain, to warn him of the impudence of the move he contemplated.

"We'll never be able to climb the cliff, Sire. My father himself died when he tried to scale these heights—and just to make it harder, those damned Bretons have built a high wall at the top of the slope."

"Nevertheless, that is how it is to be done," answered De Carteret angrily. "There's nothing to be afraid of in a wall, so long as there isn't anybody behind it. If you're afraid, you may stay aboard with your sweetheart. I thought I had taken two men on ship; I see now that I brought two mice in men's clothing, unless perhaps they're just poltroons, which is very possible too."

Everybody on deck laughed and turned to look at Lucas, who blushed a fiery red at the insult. Without a word, his ax in hand, he climbed into De Carteret's boat, and Guillette, armed only with her little knife, followed him down the side of the ship. The two boats slid noiselessly up on the beach, smooth and soft at the foot of a great pointed cliff. As they landed, the fog was suddenly dissipated, and the peak above their heads, crowned by a granite wall, seemed suddenly alive with men, and glittering with muskets. Apparently the watchmen, stationed on high on misty days, had seen the Normans' approach and given

warning, for the Bretons on the hilltop lost no time
in hurling great rocks down the steep slope, wound-
ing any one who attempted the perilous ascent. And
then, brave as they were, the Normans realized the
foolhardiness of their plan, and the greater part of
them halted, ready to go down again. Above them a
great tree fell at the blows of the defenders' axes, and
as it rolled down the hillside it, too, left its wake of
destruction. At this, the men who were left set off in
haste for the boats, and Lucas, Guillette, and De Carteret, farther up the slope than any, were forced to
follow their example, for fear of being left stranded
here, helpless, without means of escape. Guillette,
borne away in the midst of the fleeing men, did not
see that Lucas, wounded by the falling tree, was rolling unconscious to the foot of the cliff. The two boats
drew off towards the big vessel, as the men leaned all
their weight upon the oars.

Then Buron's artillery came into action; a great
cannon, loaded and ready for fire, was turned upon
the fleeing ships, and when the fuse was lighted, earth
and sky rocked with a tremendous explosion which
left a thick cloud of black smoke in its wake.

When the smoke had cleared, it was evident that
the aim was wide, for instead of destroying the small

boats, it had passed over them and buried itself deep in the *Belle Henriette* herself, shattering any hope of escape in her. De Carteret barked a sharp order, and both boats veered in another direction, hoping thus to escape the second cannon explosion, obviously due to follow almost immediately.

But aiming the cannon, and readying it for firing, were not to be done quickly, and by the time the second shot rang out, the sloops were safely away. The men aboard them raised their sails, and abandoning the useless wreck of the *Belle Henriette* to the Bretons, they set off, one towards Guernsey, the other in the direction of Jersey.

ᔓ XVIII ᔓ

Lᴜᴄᴀꜱ slowly opened his eyes and heard in a daze the creaking of the oars and the sound of men's voices talking heatedly. Gradually his brain cleared, and he remembered the blow on his head, as an event of a past life. Then the conversation of the men above became intelligible to him and he listened to the argument which swayed back and forth as to who was to blame for the disastrous failure of the attempted landing.

At last one of the crew shouted, "Pardi, if the Seigneur of St. Ouen had listened to the lad from Sark and his sweetheart in breeches, we should have had more success."

In a flash Lucas' brain cleared, and remembering Guillette he forced himself to his feet, and looked round at the survivors of the attack. Asking for Guillette, he was told that she had last been seen in the melée with De Glatigny's men.

In the distance smoke and flames seemed to rise all over Sark. The Bretons had fired the gorse covering the cliffs. There seemed no chance of escape for any of the wounded.

Lucas shouted, "Why do we not return and save Guillette—we must return. Cowards you are to leave a girl alone in the hands of that rabble. Don't you know that Buron will now stay and destroy every soul on Sark to revenge himself for to-day's work?"

Hearing the raised voices, Sir Helier called to him from the stern. Lucas stumbled towards him and implored him to give the order to turn back to Sark. Sir Helier heard him, but shook his head.

"See here, my boy, we can do nothing. Our ammunition is spent, the Island is burning, no one can force a landing now. Come with us to Jersey and we will raise such a storm about this that the Queen must hear and send a frigate to blow this Buron and his Bretons to hell. You shall come with me to London and we will make a deposition to be laid before the Queen. Then you can revenge your girl as a man of spirit should."

Lucas, shattered and weak from concussion, was shaking his fist at Sark, and cursing Buron with all his vocabulary of Norman-French, when De Carteret gave the order for rum to be distributed to the men. And in a short time, all that were left of the ill-fated expedition landed in Jersey at Grève de Lecq, where Dame de Carteret, accompanied by her servants, was on the shore to greet them.

A slow and sad procession wound its way to the Manor of St. Ouen, where hot food and care and attention for the wounded was supervised by Dame de Carteret, who herself urged Sir Helier not to delay but to proceed immediately to London to crave an audience of the Queen. The following day he set out, accompanied by Lucas, for the port of St. Aubin, there to make arrangements for a ship to carry them to England.

~ XIX ~

H AD Guillette been fully aware of the fate which
had overtaken Lucas, she would have been less
sad than she was; now, knowing only that somehow
he had disappeared, she winked back the tears which
threatened and set to work to help the wounded men
in the little boat.

"Now, now, child, don't be so upset," De Glatigny
comforted her. "Don't worry about your fiancé—un-
questionably he's gone to Jersey with Sir de Carteret.
As for us, we shall soon be in Guernsey, and I'm sure
the Governor there will commend your courage when
he hears about it. Everybody at St. Pierre Port will
want to do something for you. You've been through
hard times; now you're going to be honored."

"Oh, Sire, I wish I could believe you. But something tells me that he never left Sark—that he's lying dead there somewhere. 'If you hear bells, by night, upon the sea, prepare your soul for death right speedily.' "

Towards the middle of the morning, the sloop reached the little island of Château-Cornet, whose watch-towered walls defended the entrance to St. Pierre Port from seaward. De Glatigny, shouting to shore for the whereabouts of the Governor, learned that he was in conference with the Bailiff and the Provost at the Fort, and it seemed wise to take Guillette with him when he made his immediate report of what had happened.

"His Excellency is very busy," said the officer on duty, "and I'm afraid he can't be disturbed. Nevertheless, I'll tell him you are here, and anxious to see him."

De Glatigny and the girl waited for a few moments in the inside court, until, at last, the officer came back and led them into a great hall, with trophy-covered walls and a massive fireplace, atop which the rose stone bust of Queen Elizabeth smiled down on the game of chess in lively progress before her. The Governor, splendid in velvet, was just arguing over a move with the satin-clad Bailiff, while behind the players the Provost did his best to judge fairly between the Norman and the Englishman. Two guards by the door were absorbed in the Governor's game, too—they bent casqued heads to watch as they leaned upon their halberds crossed in the open door.

"Check to your queen," said the Bailiff, moving a castle forward.

"Very well, Bailiff—but I'll huff your pawn."

"Oh, Excellency, we're playing chess, not draughts. We don't huff when we play chess. Really, it's not the custom at all."

"Would you presume, Bailiff, to teach *me* the rules of chess? Our sovereign, the gracious Queen of England, says to me often, 'Hawthorn, my friend . . .'"

"I'm very sorry, Excellency," put in the Provost, "here in Norman country, we don't care two pins what the Queen of England—God bless her—has to say about such things. But if you were to tell us what is my lady the Duchess of Normandy's opinion . . ."

De Glatigny interrupted the conversation with a discreet cough, and the three men raised their heads.

"Oh dear, dear, dear. What a nice-looking little creature! See, Bailiff, what a charming child it is, with the old gentleman. What do you want, child—and first tell me, are you boy or girl?"

"Sire," interposed De Glatigny, "I have the profound regret to inform you that Sir Helier de Carteret, commander of the *Belle Henriette*, has failed in his plan to land on Sark. Our ship was shattered by a cannon-ball, and we were forced to abandon her. Many of the men of Jersey were killed and I have brought back our detachment, lacking five men, who were crushed by rocks. Three others have been crippled, and . . ."

"Oh, sir, spare me all the sad details. The men of Jersey are the business of the Governor of that Island," interrupted the Governor. "Unfortunately I must admit that I am not much surprised by your news, because I was sure it was impossible to take Sark. But what on earth were you doing with a pretty young girl like this in a fight like that?"

Guillette knelt before the three men and gazed up at them with her gray-velvet eyes. "Sire," she said softly, "I beseech you on my knees to send an expedition to Sark. The men who fought this morning were magnificently brave, they had a splendid leader —and a splendid lieutenant, too—but they couldn't possibly have succeeded. It cannot be done, to climb the Derrible cliff; I knew it at the time. Arm a new ship—it doesn't have to be a big one, just a little, little one—and give me just six men. I'll show them the way, and I promise you that I'll deliver the Island—and my betrothed as well."

The Governor spluttered with rage, and his face grew red. "See here, Bailiff," he roared, "is this girl mad, or am I? Not only does she criticize Sir de Carteret's plans, but she has the unmitigated impudence to suggest that she could manage it better—take command of a boat and sail over there to rescue her sweetheart. In the first place, who let her in here? Doesn't she know that no woman is allowed in the Fortress? Guards, throw her into the lockup. She shall stay there a week, as an example."

"Your pardon, Excellency," interrupted De Glatigny. "I must ask your understanding. During the battle this girl bore herself in a manner above praise, and now you wish to punish her for a crime she did not commit, because it was I who begged her to come here with me. Stay on your knees, child, and say after me: '*Haro, haro, haro, mon Prince. On me fait tort!*' Then say your Paternoster. . . . The Bailiff and the Provost, who know the Norman custom, will be your witnesses, and I'll be your sponsor. I am sure that the Duchess will grant you justice when she hears your cry of Haro. . . . Meanwhile, according to law, you

are perfectly free, and no guard will touch you, because it would go ill with him if he did."

With a sharp blow of his fist the Governor
smashed over his chess table. "May the devil take
every last one of you, you with your Paternosters. Sark
is impregnable from every side, and the devil himself couldn't get in unless he went in a coffin. Go there
with him if you like, but by all that's holy, don't come
back here again. I'm going to supper. Gentlemen,
good night."

And he stomped out of the room, shaking with
anger.

~ XX ~

I N HIGH STREET, the busiest of St. Pierre Port, a copper dish, signifying a barber, hung below a sign which bore these words:

> *At the service of elegant Guernsey people*
> JOSEPH BELLOISEAU
> *Master-barber, surgeon, leech*
> Apothecary to the Courts of France and England

Outside a tablet announced the current prices:

> For trimming hair, beard, and nails
>   in the Parisian style——   5 deniers
> For bleeding, leeches, removing
>   corns and teeth——   4 deniers
> For foot-baths, sitz-baths, purging,
>   enema——   3 deniers
> For trimming cat or dog——   2 deniers
> Unguents, pomades, soaps, and ointments,
>   priced according to quality.

Inside the dark little shop, its walls hung with the dried skins of snakes and wildcats, cluttered with tables and stools, Belloiseau and his assistants hastened to wait upon their customers, while Léonie, Belloiseau's wife, a Parisian, prepared remedies on a counter laden with pottery jars, bearing names like: Diascordium—Catholicon—Oryx—Scordium—Cassia lignea—Anome—Cardamome—Malabathrum.

Perched on high stools at tables weighted with cider jugs and flasks of burnt wine, half a dozen clients were awaiting the attention of the Master, who, in a butcher's apron and a tall white cap, followed by an assistant carrying his implements, walked from one to the other of his patients, bleeding this one, extracting a molar from that, thrusting his thumb into the cheek of still another, pulling taut the skin to be shaved. He removed the corns of an apoplectic animal-merchant, carried a home-compounded remedy to a sufferer from catarrh, fetched more medicines from Madame Léonie's counter.

A small dog, clipped to look like a baby lion, chased one of the assistants around the room, and jumped at last into a customer's foot-bath, while a new-comer prepared for his treatment in a wooden booth protected from view by a green baize curtain.

It had begun to rain outside in large slow drops, and from time to time village women, as eager perhaps for a moment of shelter as to sell the wares in their baskets, thrust hooded heads through the door and sang,

> "Lovely lobsters, mackerel to fry,
>   They will delight, if you'll only buy";

or

> "I have apples, peaches, pears—
>   Mine are better than any of theirs";

or

> "Come and taste of the sweet fresh milk,
>   As white as snow, as smooth as silk."

The milkwoman's low-cut dress, her plump shoulders, brought forth compliments from all the men in the shop save one; he, surveying his small elegant beard in the hand-mirror the barber gave him, did not deign to watch the vulgar scene before him. Instead, he gave his attention to Belloiseau, who was now preparing to cut his hair in the latest Parisian style, speaking no word to the barber, merely indicating by signs what he wished done.

"Now, Monsieur would doubtless like a pleasant-smelling lotion, then a good hot bath, scented with calambac. And after that, a little glass of Damascus water, perhaps. There's nothing so good for you, to drive away disease and stir up all the functions of the body. Shall I give the sign to have your bath-water heated?"

The stranger shook his head, and the barber, some-what taken aback, went on, "Of course, it is as Monsieur wishes; I won't urge him. Not every one is fond of these new styles. Doubtless Monsieur is a foreigner. English or French, perhaps?"

"Flemish."

"Oh, yes, of course. I'm not at all surprised. People come to me from every corner of the earth, nowadays, because of my fame. Why, only the other day Madame Tassine de Gouberville came all the way from her manor near Coutances to try to find out from my wife the secret of the permanent curls that I introduced in 1558, when our good Duchess was crowned Queen of England. Even the Princess Gaud in Sark, who is Buron's mistress as everybody knows, has adopted them, it seems. . . ."

"Gaud isn't really a princess," put in a fat man. "She's only a clever young trollop. Why, she was wearing the prostitute's red bow on her shoulder when she first met Buron in a pleasure-house in St.

Malo. He had just come back from ten years in the King of France's galleys, and not as a guard, either, believe you me. He was chained hand and foot, because he tried to murder the Count of Luzarches when he was his valet."

"All the same, he's ruler in Sark now, and he gave those sailors on the *Belle Henriette* the shock of their lives. He turned the tables on them, all right—surprised them when they expected to surprise him."

"Does that astonish you?" asked the man in the sitz-bath. "Don't forget that those caves in Sark are full of Spanish treasure. They say that Buron has promised to send a diamond as big as a pigeon's egg to the Governor of Guernsey every year, in return for his protection, so that the English fleet won't interfere. I have it from my wife—it's the truth. Because after all, if any one really wanted to get rid of them . . ."

"What a shame that you haven't time to take it up yourself, Babylas," chuckled a man who was having a tooth pulled. "You could free Sark with a flick of the wrist, and make your fortune at the same time, with all those jewels you were talking about."

"And the next day we could all look out and watch Gaud being taken to the pillory, as naked as a child, thrown across a donkey's back. I reserve one of your windows for that day, Belloiseau."

"Is it true," asked the Master-barber as he heated his curling iron, "that she paints her toe-nails red?"

Every one roared with laughter at this question.

"Sure and certain," answered the voice of the man in the bath. "She even has herself shaved under the arms."

"Oh, Babylas—that's too much. Did your wife tell you that?"

"No, I got that from her maid, Jacotte."

"But, after all, how does she happen to know so much?"

Just then the door opened, and Guillette, drenched to the skin, stood on the threshold. Conversation stopped abruptly, and every one turned to stare at her, for she was an odd sight in her dripping fisherman's clothes.

"Is Monsieur Belloiseau here, please?" she timidly inquired.

"At your service," answered the barber.

"Sir, my name is Guillonne, but everybody in Sark calls me Guillette. Have you by any chance seen Gilles the fisherman, or your cousin Catherine, his wife?

They tried to escape from Sark several days ago, and they thought to come here."

"Oh, my dear child! So you are Catherine's daughter. No, I haven't seen her yet. But tell me, are you a boy, that you're wearing breeches? Come and kiss me all the same!"

Léonie left her counter and came over to look more closely at the pretty girl, and the customers and assistants clustered about her, while the man behind the curtain in his bath stood up and stretched his neck to get a better view of her gray eyes.

"I hope you'll stay with us until you find your parents," went on Belloiseau. "There's a nice little room right next to ours, and you can be very useful here in the shop . . . can't she, Léonie? By the way, we were just talking about Gaud. You've just come from Sark —have you ever seen her?"

"What's the matter with you, Joseph?" Léonie interrupted dryly. "You know very well that leeches aren't allowed to have young girls in the house. Don't listen to him, Miss. You don't belong here. You'd best go to the Convent at Anneville and ask Reverend Mother to put you up there. She'll be glad to see you; she'll give you some fancywork to do to earn your keep. Good-by, Miss."

And Guillette, not anxious to urge the barber to take her in, passed through the circle of men who stared curiously at her, out the door of the shop, and in the pouring rain turned her weary steps up High Street.

ᥲ XXI ᥲ

IN THE main square of town, before the sign of the
Siren Tavern which displayed a beguiling mermaid,
Guillette found a noisy crowd, all eager like herself
to find some shelter under the porch from the torren-
tial rain. In the center of the crowd three men and a
woman, tired and hoarse, sang and played, evidently
hoping to stir the generosity of the passers-by. Their
instruments were out of tune and the woman's voice
was thick with unshed tears, but the notes of their
song reminded Guillette of the day, so short a time
ago, when she had been so happy, when, from her
home on the cliff, she had heard Lucas' voice and
those of her father and brothers mingled in the plaintive song the woman sang now:

"In Coutances in Normandy,
St. Elias and St. Hilary,
Kneeling pious, raise their plea. . . ."

"Kind sirs," sniffled the woman, "be generous towards the poor fugitives who have been driven out of Sark from fear of Buron. If you have no money, throw us at least a crust of bread, so that we won't starve."

As she finished her speech, Guillette noticed a young man approaching, a young man whose sugarloaf hat and elegant silver-striped cloak proclaimed very clearly that he was no native of Guernsey. As he drew closer, she realized that she had seen him at the barber's; that he had been having his hair cut while she was there.

He took off his hat and bowed low. "Since you are on your way to the Convent, my child, perhaps I may walk a little way with you, to be sure that you reach your destination safely. I saw you a few moments back, in your cousins' shop. Allow me to introduce myself. I am the Chevalier Van den Schreyer, captain of the Flemish brig *Zuyderzee,* which you may see over there, in port, on its way from the West Indies. Isn't there something I can do for you?"

"Alas, sir! I'm afraid not," with a wry smile. "That is, unless you'd care to deliver Sark."

"I'm afraid that's a dangerous venture, but perhaps it's not impossible. My crew held out against pirates in the Caribbean, and they're not cowards. Is it true that there is untold treasure hidden in those caves?"

"I've seen it myself. I've touched the cases that hold it—all those coins, and those priceless jewels."

"Not one of all those gaping fools at Belloiseau's just now thought to ask you whether you're hungry or thirsty. Wouldn't it be a good idea to step into this tavern, out of this horrible rain, and have something to eat, while you tell me how this cave may be reached?"

He pushed open the door of the Siren, and they stepped into a great paneled room, badly lighted by red and green glass windows. When the servant had brought a fresh white table-cloth, the stranger ordered dinner for them both—ormers, a savory stew, two tankards of light foaming ale. Guillette ate ravenously, so intent upon the good hot food that she had small time for polite conversation. When she had finished her sweet, she looked up, to see with astonishment that the rain had stopped and that the minstrels outside had gone on their way. But Van den Schreyer, noticing that she seemed a little less sad, continued to ply her with questions.

It was only when night had fallen at last that they rose from the table, and set out once more on the road to the Convent, through tiny dark winding streets.

"I think your plan excellent, and well worthy of a true Norman," he went on as they walked. "With God's help, we'll succeed. But what is more important than all the jewels in Sark is the chance that if I try the plan, I may be able to bring back a smile to your lovely, unhappy eyes."

Guillette stopped suddenly.

"Then I must tell you, sir, that my eyes will be truly happy only when they look into those of my betrothed, who disappeared in the battle this morning."

Van den Schreyer sighed sadly and looked at the girl without a word. They were at the Convent door, and the Fleming had seized the knocker, before either of them spoke again. Guillette said, looking into his admiring eyes with her own honest ones, "Can you give me your word as a gentleman, sir, that you will hope for nothing, expect nothing, except the jewels and the gold that we were talking about a while ago, as your reward?"

He said nothing, but continued to gaze into her eyes. She put out her hand and let fall the knocker herself. "Answer me," she said in a low voice. "I cannot follow you if you have any other thought."

He seized her hand and carried it to his lips. Already the corner of the Sister Guest-Mistress' coif showed white at the grille in the door.

"No other thought," he said humbly. "I'll swear it because you ask, painful as it is to me. You have my word of honor. In the next few weeks I will make every effort to equip my ship with muskets and ammunition, and then you shall come aboard and we'll set sail—and if all goes well you'll be in Sark once more."

"In Sark in a few weeks," Guillette repeated, soft as an echo, as she watched the young man's back retreating down the dark little street. "God grant that the one I love may still be there."

ᔥᔤ XXII ᔤᔥ

IN THE great refectory of the Monastery, Gaud and
Buron, at table, prepared to dine upon a magnificent lobster, such as may be found only on the rocks
of Sark. From time to time Buron threw a malevolent
glance at Gaud's scarred face, while she, apparently
indifferent, tossed scraps of food to the monkey
perched not far away, and to the dog at her feet. She
smiled at the tinkling sound of her golden bracelets,
and carefully avoiding Buron's eye did her best to
ignore his unpleasant looks.

Both of them had been in exceedingly bad humor
since the unfortunate evening not long ago when
Buron had waited in vain for Guillette's return, and
Gaud, on the other hand, locked up in her damp
prison, had been forced to wait for Rosario to free

herself from her own bonds and come to set her at liberty. And the victory over De Carteret, which might have given them common ground for rejoicing, served only to start another honey-voiced argument.

"Why did you have to take all those prisoners?" asked Gaud, breaking the heavy silence at last. "Don't you know, my sweet, that there are already more people here than we've food for, and that flour is beginning to run low?"

Buron dipped the claw of his lobster in his sauce dish.

"Everybody eats too much anyway," he observed sententiously.

"Oh, admit that you hoped that one or another of the prisoners could tell you something about that little vermin to whom you wanted to give my clothes the other night. I have to laugh whenever I think how you were taken in by her declarations of love. You must have been bewitching when you were young, before you lost your eye. But now! But you must have a soft heart, after all, in spite of your fierce airs, to be taken in by that chit!"

"While we're speaking of that, how about you, my lovely? You must be pretty romantic yourself, to tell me you were sick abed, and then to go and spend the

Port du Moulin

By J. M. W. Turner

night, with a ball and chain on your foot, in that dark cave, and to come back with that delightful welt across your face. Anyway, it's ridiculous to speak of a soft heart in connection with any one who's nick-named the Destroyer."

"A nickname doesn't mean a thing, my love, especially when one has chosen it oneself. Anyway, how do you know that you don't have other nicknames that you've never even heard?"

"Perhaps they call me the Protector of the Poor? My astrologer tells me that I shall die in the skin of a saint," murmured Buron, knocking wood.

"No, he didn't say in the skin, he said in the tomb of a saint, my darling."

"That's ridiculous. Nobody dies in a tomb! Oh, and remember what he said about you—immediately after I die, you'll be abducted by a great black beast who breathes fire and smoke."

"Now that, I grant you, *is* ridiculous. Anyway, thank God it's not to-day nor to-morrow. We'll have plenty of time to worry about it later. In any case, my jade talisman will protect me——"

"Take care you do not lose it."

A messenger stepped up to Buron, a folded note in his hand.

"Sire, a Flemish brig is crossing the Port du Moulin. They sent in a little boat, and left this note in a flask on the rocks."

"Give it to me."

"Perhaps it's a note from your little sweetheart," Gaud mocked. "No doubt she has written to tell you how much she loves you, and when she'll be back."

Buron opened the letter, and tracing each line with his finger, read aloud, with considerable difficulty:

"The Chevalier Van den Schreyer, captain of the *Zuyderzee* out of Flushing, sends his most courteous compliments to the Lord of Bruel, Marquis of Rosporden, Ruler by the Grace of God of the Island of Sark, and begs his leave to recount the following:

"Monseigneur Alvinius, Bishop of Bruges, has just died aboard his ship, returning from a pilgrimage to Mont St. Michel, made in fulfilment of a vow.

"Before he died, Monseigneur the Bishop, whose last moments were particularly painful because of the lack of any spiritual comfort, begged the Chevalier Van den Schreyer to spare him the last humiliation of a burial at sea.

"He exacted a solemn oath that his body be interred in the crypt of the Sanctuary of St. Magloire, as near as possible to the tomb of the Saint. If M. de Rosporden grants his kind permission to the Chevalier to carry out this oath, the Chevalier would be most honored if the Marquis and his men would attend the funeral feast, to take place at sunset before the Sanctuary.

"VAN DEN SCHREYER"

Buron and Gaud stared at one another.

"We couldn't possibly refuse a request like that," said Buron, licking his lips at the thought of the feast.

"True enough," answered Gaud, less enthusiastically. "But you don't want to fall into a trap, either. Is it your idea to seize the brig before the funeral, or after?"

Buron thought for a moment.

"During the funeral," he said simply. "Take a pen and this vellum and write my answer."

"The Marquis of Rosporden, Commander-at-Arms of the Island of Sark, thanks the Chevalier Van den Schreyer for his great courtesy. He considers it a sacred duty to help him, inasmuch as he is able, to carry out the dying wishes of the holy Prelate. He accepts with great pleasure the invitation to be present with his men at the funeral feast.

"In order that his homage rendered to the memory of the dead should in no way lose its purely peaceful and religious nature, it is requested that the men who come ashore from the *Zuyderzee* should carry no arms whatsoever, and that Captain Van den Schreyer will agree to an armed guard to watch over the cannons of the brig until the return of her sailors."

When Buron had finished dictating this reply, he made ready to sign it, but Gaud stopped him.

"And the tariffs?" she asked.

"What tariffs?"

"It would look much better, much more natural. Wait a minute . . ."

She took up her quill pen and added:

In order to defray the expenses of the funeral, the Chevalier Van den Schreyer will kindly be ready to pay upon landing,

for landing tax——	10 sols tournois
for tomb and inscription——	5 sols tournois
for the Mass, the candles, and the incense——	2 sols tournois
for the sexton——	1 denier

"Is there anything more?"

Buron, about to sign, hesitated. "Wait a second," he said. "You forgot the feast. Write:

duty on food and drink——	10 sols tournois
placing of benches and tables——	5 sols tournois
lights——	2 sols tournois
for the poor——	1 denier

What else has been forgotten? Can you think of anything?"

"Not at the moment," said Gaud. "Here, make your mark right by my finger."

ᔥᔥ XXIII ᔥᔥ

Buron's conditions had been accepted without demur, and so it was that the setting sun illumined two small boats from the *Zuyderzee* plying their way ashore, manned by eight Flemings, unarmed as Buron had ordered, laden with the coffin of the Prelate as well as with barrels of food and wine. Next to the coffin huddled the Bishop's page, so engrossed with grief that he could not take his handkerchief away from his tearful face.

Before they were admitted to the natural passageway which led from the harbor to the rest of the Island, the men had to submit to a thorough search, and Van den Schreyer was obliged to pay the tariff, which he did very graciously. When the *Zuyderzee's* boats sailed back to the bay, they were manned by eight Bretons, well armed, chosen from Buron's most faithful followers.

On the Island, the procession set out, headed by the coffin borne on the Flemings' shoulders, while Van den Schreyer and Buron, in deep mourning, followed behind, and the little page, still flooded with tears, brought up the rear.

A little behind them came Bretons carrying the provisions: tongue, ham, anchovies, salmon, all sorts of succulent spice cakes. To assuage the thirst that these foods could not but arouse, there were bottles of red wine, a cask of the best Jamaica rum, and several flasks of old Holland gin. In order that nothing be lacking, Van den Schreyer had provided in addition clay pipes and a package of the odorous herb which was beginning to be popular in Europe under the name of "Queen's herb," and which the Antillean Indians called "tobacco."

It was almost dark by the time the two groups reached the Sanctuary, and through its half-opened door could be seen the pin-points of flame upon the altar candles inside. While the mournful dirge of the bells filled the dusk, Father Samson on the threshold, somber in his funeral robes, waited for the dead priest.

In the darkness, too, the torches which lit the long tables set with goblets outside the church, cast strange shadows on the helmets of the noisy soldiers who were already seated, saving places in spite of altercations for their comrades who had risen to fetch food for them. Even the Flemings, having deposited their sad burden, mingled for a moment with the hilarious throng, pausing to empty a glass of rum, or to offer a cigar. But it was not long before another order came, and lifting the coffin to their shoulders, they followed Father Samson and Van den Schreyer through the shadowed nave and down into the crypt.

In the excitement nobody had noticed the little page, who had left the funeral party. As for Buron, he sat down with his men, and gave no thought to anything more serious than his self-imposed task of emptying the flagons of rum before him as fast as they were filled. Thus it was that the strangers went alone into the church.

The Flemings laid down their burden on a bier surrounded with candles in the middle of the crypt, in front of the Saint's tomb. There was a dull sound in the coffin as they set it down, and almost immediately, another sound—that of the church doors grinding closed, as Buron had ordered.

"Well, my children," said Van den Schreyer softly, rubbing his hands together, "everything seems to have worked out very well so far. By the way, Mademoiselle Guillette, allow me to congratulate you on an excellent plan—*and* a very fine performance," he laughed as the "page-boy" pulled off her blonde wig, and shook her own dark curls with a merry smile.

The lifted lid of the coffin disclosed, not the sainted remains of the dead Prelate, but instead a dazzling array of arms: eight arquebuses, complete with powder-horns, bullets, as well as with swords, spears, and other weapons which would do their work silently. The Flemings lifted them out, and, by the light of two flaming torches, red and brilliant in the crypt's dimness, lifted the trap-door and went after Guillette down the narrow ladder which led to the secret catacombs below.

❦ XXIV ❧

G AUD had been present at the arrival of the funeral party, and something in the little page-
boy's figure had caught her eye. It took more than a
wig to hide from her the fact that this was the de-
spised Guillette.

She thought that Lucas had no doubt escaped her,
and she set out furiously in search of him. The fact
that the church doors were closed after the visitors,
and guards posted outside, added to her irritation,
and she walked towards the smaller sacristy door, left
unguarded now. On tiptoe she went down into the
crypt, drawing back in astonishment and a presage of
fear when she realized that the coffin was open and
empty, and the Flemings vanished. She whirled

around at a light sound behind her, only to stare
aghast into Buron's burning eyes.

"You bitch," he shouted, grabbing her throat, "now
you can't deny that you've betrayed me. Where did
those men go?"

"You're drunk, Buron. You don't even remember
your own orders. I knew that that was your Guillette,
with those foreigners. Where have they gone now?"

"My Guillette? My Guillette was here? Oh, I didn't
know—I didn't know."

"You lie, you swine. Lucas was with her, and
you've murdered them both!"

Buron seized this opportunity to have a subtle and
devastating revenge upon Gaud. "All right, I admit
it. I followed your advice: no quarter. After all, you
were right when you said we had plenty of mouths to
feed, without taking any more prisoners. If you go
down to the oubliette, you'll find them both in the
well. Poor Gaud, you don't have very good luck in
your love affairs either, in spite of your jade talisman."

"Murderer!"

"Harlot!"

Gaud seized her tiny dagger, called ' misericord"
because it was used in battle to speed the dying on

their way, and hurled herself at Buron, plunging the weapon deep into his breast, while he tried to reach her with his swordstick, his eyes hot, his breath heavy as that of a great beast. But he was too late; Gaud's dagger was buried deep, and his blood spurted out in great red drops, staining the stone floor with crimson patches. With a last effort he tried to stand erect; instead his legs buckled under him, and he fell headlong into the Saint's open tomb, only his feet projecting wildly into the air, waving frantically.

Gaud turned to rush upstairs, unmindful of the funeral taper which had fallen over during the struggle, whose flames even now licked hungrily at the Marquis' boots, filling the crypt with a sickening odor.

In the bell-tower the dirge went on, but now a new sound mingled with it: the drunken songs of the carousing Bretons had turned into screams of pain, as musket shots rang sharp and sudden through the night.

~ XXV ~

PRESENTLY the Flemings came out of the Monastery. The abbey ruins seemed to them peopled with strange dark shadows—but no sign of living people. Where were the Sark folk that Guillette had promised would assist them? The little group went silently forward, the tips of their arquebuses shining like stars in the darkness. At the Tithebarn of St. Eustace they found the Bretons, drunken with rum, and overcome with the unaccustomed fumes of tobacco, lying senseless across the tables or rolling on the ground.

Suddenly Guillette shouted, as arranged, the old war-cry of the Normans, "Dieu Aide!" and they threw themselves upon the Bretons, literally tearing them to pieces. There were screams, the dull thud of bodies falling to the ground, the crack of splintering bones, and sometimes, when a Breton offered too much resistance, a flash of fire and the whirr of a bullet.

Meantime Guillette and a few others managed to force open the church portals, and seizing the bell-ropes, pulled and pulled, until the bell in the tower above sang out the joyful news of the Island's deliverance. Then, her sight sated with bloodshed, she glimpsed a narrow stream of smoke pouring up from the crypt, and thinking it curious, raced down, to find a body wrapped in flames, blazing in the Saint's tomb. It was burned past recognition, but she did not doubt that it was the Saint come back to his rightful resting-place.

"St. Magloire took pity on us. He has come back to his tomb. Buron is gone; so is Gaud. God has come to the aid of the Flemings, and Sark is free!"

Escaping from the scenes around, Guillette dashed away to the Écluse, to find it empty and deserted. Then, her heart beating wildly with dread, and noting signs of destruction everywhere, she found her way through the desolate and burnt-out cliff path to her old home.

At the Éperquerie, as she approached it, her heart

L'Écluse

sank. No sign of life anywhere, the door off its hinges and part of the roof burnt away. Calling, "Father—Mother! Oh, God, where are you? Have we come too late?" she sank on the disordered green bed and gave way to a paroxysm of tears.

Suddenly she raised her head. She had heard a faint sound, and her name barely whispered. Starting to her feet in fear, she saw the iron door of the big stone baking-oven in the wall of the hearth, slowly opening, and with a leap of her heart, she recognized her mother's face inside. With difficulty Catherine crawled out of the oven and clung pitifully to Guillette, shuddering and weeping, on the point of collapse, while her daughter held her close in her strong young arms as if she could not bear to let her go.

"Where is Father—and Lucas?"

"The Bretons sank your father by throwing stones in his boat when he tried to take Coryse and Douce-Marie away. They were all drowned."

"And Lucas?"

"God knows, my child. Is he not with you?"

Guillette's eyes filled with tears. She had to bite her lip to keep it steady, but seeing her mother's distress, she said nothing. The old woman, for so she now seemed, could only repeat, "All are dead, all, all. . . ."

ᔥ XXVI ᔫ

THE soldiers who had been sent aboard the *Zuy-derzee* received a very hearty welcome. The search for cannon on her decks of course proved no more than a farce; there was not one aboard, and everybody knew it. But if they failed to find arms, they did find something more to their taste—a table spread with all the succulent and exotic delicacies brought back from the Indies; enough to make the mouth water, and beside them, displayed to their view, and to quench the thirst the high-seasoned foods would produce, a huge cask of admirable wine.

The Negro ccok was the only member of the expedition left aboard, and at first, seeing his enormous black face, the glittering whites of his rolling eyes, the soldiers held back, thinking that here surely was the devil in person and no mistake. But as they saw how stupid he was, they grew more and more bold, and, at length sitting down at the table, they began to demand his services on behalf of their empty stomachs. When they had eaten and drunk liberally, those who had brought cards along began to play with them, while the others contented themselves with rolling dice. Little by little the slow magic of the wine, heavily drugged in accordance with Van den Schreyer's orders, began to take effect, and it was not long before the invaders were all sound asleep, tearing the ship apart with their drunken snores.

Boulou, the cook, did as he had been told. He searched them immediately for arms, throwing those he found upon them in a heap on the table, and, working slowly and deliberately, bound the soldiers securely hand and foot, with a heavy cord. When he had finished this task, he took up his strange, three-stringed instrument, and in a voice thick with homesickness began to sing songs of his own making about his faraway native land, songs that were half dirges and half passionate outcries against the fate which had brought him to so distant a place.

When he had finished the tune, he crossed to the ship's rail, and watching the black waves below him, he listened to the night sounds. Far away he heard the noise of shouting, of shots, and then, like a strange counterpoint, the joyous melody of church bells. . . .

Suddenly a sound closer at hand caught his ear, the steady rhythm of oars cutting through the water. A moment later he glimpsed a small boat hastening to the side of the ship where he stood. He watched, startled, as two young women climbed up the rope ladder. One of them was dark and handsome, and she carried a tiny gray monkey, small as a new-born child, in her arms. The other, very blonde, very pale, wore a blood-stained gown; it was Gaud, her hands still warm and red with Buron's newly shed blood. When she stepped on the deck, her eyes encountered those of the great sullen black man, and she drew back instinctively, for the cigar in his thick-lipped mouth threw an eerie red glow over his shining ebony face. She watched with terror as he puffed the cigar; here, surely, was the fire-breathing monster of whom the astrologer had warned her.

Then her glance, passing over the sleeping Bretons, was caught by the gleam of their weapons spread out on the table.

"Shipmates?" she questioned, pointing to them with trembling fingers.

"No, prisoners," answered the Negro proudly.

"What are you going to do with them?"

This was an unexpected question, and he was not sure what answer he should give. He shrugged his shoulders, and thought for a moment. Then, "Cut off their heads. To-morrow morning!" he cried.

"Are you alone here?" The young woman looked around the brig.

He laughed delightedly. "All alone, with them." Then, like the poet he was, he elaborated imaginatively, "I, Captain. They, sailors. You two, pretty passengers. Captain's friends." And after a minute, he added pleasantly, pointing to the monkey in Rosario's arms, "Pretty little girl with her mama."

Gaud's eyes shone and she smiled. Unfastening her magnificent ruby-and-sapphire necklace to which her jade talisman was attached, she put it around the Negro's neck, and he, watching fascinated, grinned with pleasure.

"To bring luck to Boulou—never sick, never die?"

"Pretty passengers, good friends of the kind Captain," Gaud said softly. "They'd love to go for a little trip. Why not now?"

Boulou stared fatuously at the two young women, and, as he pictured scenes of orgies to himself, his

lips broke into a grin that seemed to split his face
from ear to ear.

"Good to go now," he answered, putting his clumsy
arm around the blonde woman's waist.

"We must wake up the crew," she smiled, slipping
out of his reach.

And she began to shake the sleeping men, slapping
them, undoing their bonds, until, still drugged as they
were, they staggered to their feet and clustered around
her. Then she seized a whistle from the table, and in
a harsh voice very different to the one the Negro had
heard her use before, she shouted, "Follow me. Make
ready to lift anchor. Raise the topman. Hoist the top-
gallant. Steersman, to the wheel, head for St. Malo."

"Head for no place at all." Rosario's voice was
calm. "All the sails are in the sea, and it'll be hours
before they're dry enough to hoist. The helm is locked
up, too. . . ."

Gaud hesitated. Then, suddenly, turning towards
Boulou, she cried, "This black pig made fun of us.
Throw him into the sea—that's all he deserves."

Then her glance fell upon the wine-cask, and she
changed her mind. "No, perhaps he can still be useful to us. Chain him up in the empty barrel, and if his
friends follow us, throw it into the sea. They'll stop

to pick him up, and it will make them slacken their speed."

The men hastened to seize the Negro. "First, give me back my talisman—he won't need it in the wine keg," she added.

While this was going on, Rosario was struggling with the monkey, Chimène, whom she was trying to hold as a prisoner in her arms. Gaud's devotion to the little animal was such that she had insisted on its being brought on board with her. With a final struggle the monkey leapt from Rosario's arms to the deck, and there it proceeded to imitate a Spanish dance that it had seen Rosario execute, holding up its little hands as if it held castanets.

One of the men tore the necklace from the Negro's neck, and held it out to Gaud, but Rosario seized it instead.

"This necklace belongs to me," she said shortly. "Buron promised it to me while he was alive, and now that he's dead, I certainly intend to have it."

The Bretons stared at her open-mouthed. It was the first word they had had of the death of their leader.

"It's true," she said. "You didn't know that he was dead, did you? Well, look at this woman; see how she's spattered with blood? That's Buron's blood.

She's just murdered him—or anyway, that's what she told me when she begged me to escape with her. But I know something else, too—even if she did forget to tell me: the Governor of Guernsey offered her pardon and a hundred pounds if she turned you over to him, now that your leader is dead. Right this minute ships are waiting for you between Jersey and Guernsey, with Helier de Carteret as their captain. Do as you like. As for me, I'm not going to risk my neck by staying aboard this brig one minute longer; not while this she-devil is here." As she spoke, she was adjusting the necklace, and now that it was in place, she stepped aside, and, studying her reflection in the little mirror which hung at her belt, she smiled with pleasure at her image there.

The men were struck dumb. Gaud, who grew paler and paler, seemed at the end of her strength. How could she possibly hope to exonerate herself of these accusations, half-true, half-fantastic, delivered in a voice so quiet that it might have been commenting on the pleasant weather.

"Where can you go?" she pleaded. "We daren't go back to Sark—they'd make short work of us there, now that our men are all dead, and the natives in revolt."

Rosario held out an arm to the east. The first streaks of dawn shot across the horizon, above the dark outlines of the Norman coast.

"If we went in the little boat, we could reach the Cotentin in just a few hours," she said. "The French are hospitable, they would take us in. We could tell them that our brig was shipwrecked on the reefs. Then we could walk up to Brittany, around the Bay of St. Michel. It's the only way we can get away from Helier de Carteret. But this woman must be punished for her treason. I, for one, refuse to take her with us. . . ."

Immediately the soldiers turned on Gaud, their eyes blazing.

"Put her to death, the viper."

"Let her die."

"Fasten her up in the barrel with the Negro. They ought to get along together very well."

"Let's throw them both into the sea. The current will carry them away."

And in an instant, the woman, bound hand and foot, was thrown into the barrel with the black, who grimaced with terror.

When the cask was just about to be hurled overboard, a Breton grabbed Chimène from the deck and thrust her into the barrel between the black man and the woman.

"Let's throw in the monkey for good measure. He'll amuse them during the trip. By heaven, when the devil sees them at the gates of hell, he won't know what to make of it. He'll think that's the child of the household. . . ."

The keg splashed into the sea, and the spray it cast up washed over the gunwale. Although the current was northward, the Bretons followed Rosario's advice, and having taken their directions, set off towards Cotentin, without so much as a glance at the *Zuyderzee,* riding pleasantly at anchor in the first gold rays of the morning sun.

ᔓ XXVII ᔒ

A T St. Pierre Port in Guernsey, in the Court
House, the officials were gathered together. The
Governor in his scarlet uniform sat in his big arm-
chair opposite the Deputies from the whole Island
gathered here, and next to him sat the Provost and
the Bailiff, equally splendid in purple robes edged
with ermine. De Carteret stood erect before them all,
his blue and golden cloak thrown back over his shoulder, his hand firm on his stock. Behind him, lost in
the shadows, Lucas listened as the Governor spoke.

"Sir, the messenger who summoned you from Jersey must have told you that this meeting was an ex-
tremely important one. My gracious Sovereign grows
more and more displeased daily by the condition of
Sark, which has been for so long a hideaway for

thieves, pirates, and other wrong-doers; she has
thought it well to put an end to this state of affairs,
for the good of the other Norman islands, and their
inhabitants, her beloved subjects.

"Consequently, she has decided to make Sark a fief,
and to make you Lord of it, the title to go to your
heirs in perpetuity."

Monsieur de Carteret bowed coldly.

"The clerk will read you the letter patent which
gives you your rights. This letter is written in English
and in Latin. In which tongue do you prefer to hear
it?"

"Excellency, I should like to hear it in French—in
patois, if possible. I know little Latin and less English."

"Then it will be translated for you."

The clerk adjusted his horn-rimmed spectacles and
read: "Elizabeth, by the Grace of God Queen of England, France, and Ireland, Duchess of Normandy, to
all those to whom this letter shall come, greeting."

Every one stood up, and removed his hat.

"God bless her," they all shouted together.

"Since the Island of Sark has long since been the refuge
of thieves, pirates, and so forth [Monsieur the Governor
told you all this just now—um—yes—her beloved sub-

jects. Very well], we have decided that in return for a yearly rent of fifty sols tournois, payable at the feast of St. Michael to our Receiver General at Guernsey, and in return also for the formal employment of forty farmers as inhabitants, to be armed by you with muskets, and transported thither with their families to cultivate the earth and dwell in decent homes,

"We give and deed to our beloved Chevalier, Helier de Carteret, Lord of St. Ouen in the Island of Jersey, who accepts . . ."

"I beg your pardon, Sire," interrupted De Carteret. "I don't accept anything at all, with your kind permission."

The Governor leaped to his feet.

"What on earth are you talking about? Not accept the fief that Her Majesty wishes to give you?"

"Well, I accept and I don't accept, if you know what I mean. I wouldn't mind having that fief at all. But fifty sols, and forty farmers, and muskets, and houses—et cetera, et cetera—I think not! That's much too much to ask for an island that's still in the hands of the Bretons, that you can't even get to, and that's accursed, if what people say is true. I really wouldn't know where to get forty tenants—and anyway, Her Majesty, when she promised me the Island at her court in London, said nothing of all these conditions."

"Very well. Then I shall suggest to Her Majesty that she give it to the Bishop of Winchester, who's been begging for it."

"To an Englishman, Excellency? That would be dreadful! By what right could an Englishman command in Norman country? We both have the same sovereign, because the Normans conquered England; but the English haven't conquered Normandy yet— not that I've heard anything about. Don't forget, Sire, the King rules us only because he's the Duke, and the Queen because she's the Duchess!"

The Provost, the Bailiff, and the Deputies bowed their heads in approval at these proud words. The clerk took off his glasses and looked at the Governor, who did not try to hide his displeasure.

"Well, you might listen to the end of the charter, anyway."

"The charter, Excellency? Shouldn't we rather say, this deed full of conditions?"

The clerk went on: "We give and grant—oh yes, I read that—who accepts—hem—with the title of Seigneur of Sark, to be handed down to the eldest son or daughter, in the Norman fashion, with all the lands, prairies, pastures, mines, hidden treasures, buildings, or their materials, if in ruins, the right to make laws, levy dues, seize wreckage and salvage, mills, and watercourses."

The Jersey Seigneur opened his eyes which he had closed during the reading. He thought of the accursed isle become the happy isle, the fields heavy with golden grain, the pastures filled with sheep, and farmyards noisy with roosters' crowing. He was convinced, but still he hesitated a moment.

Just then the Captain of the Guards stepped up to the Governor. "Excellency, I have just heard that there is not a soul left on Sark. Those who brought the news are here. Shall I show them in?

"Immediately."

In an instant the officer was back with Van den Schreyer and Guillette, she in a handsome gown and lace cap, bought for her by the Fleming at a shop in St. Pierre Port.

Lucas jumped from the bench where he had been sitting and hurried towards her, his face radiant, while she, seeing him at the same moment, ran and threw herself into his arms.

The representative of the Crown glared.

"Well, what's all this? You back again? I suppose you're going to tell me you were the one who drove the Bretons out!"

Guillette's face dimpled with her wide smile, and she tossed her head. "Oh, no, sir, not all by myself I didn't. This Flemish Seigneur, and his eight sailors were with me. Buron is gone, and all the Bretons are dead, except for the few who escaped towards St. Malo with Princess Gaud. . . . The flag of Normandy has been flying everywhere on the Island for several days."

The Governor looked from one to the other of the startled magistrates beside him. Then he stood up, and with a gesture typical of him struck the table a mighty blow with his fist.

"You're lying," he shouted. "I'd have heard of it long ago, if there were an atom of truth in what you're saying."

"Excellency," said Helier de Carteret, "this girl climbed the cliff with her fiancé and me the other day. I am so sure that what she says is true that I accept now the charter you are offering me. If you'll pass it over, I'll sign it right away."

He seized the goose-quill pen from the clerk and signed his name at the foot of the paper. The Bailiff and the Provost added their names.

"One word more," said De Carteret. "I owe a great deal to my lieutenant, M. de Glatigny, and my first act as Seigneur of Sark is to appoint him Seneschal. But I owe another debt, too—to this boy," and he pointed to Lucas. "He fell at my side as we scaled the cliffs at Derrible. Luckily I was able to bring him back to Jersey. But I insulted him in public once; I called him coward and poltroon. He assures me that he doesn't hold it against me, but I want to make reparation as public as the insult was. I have already taken him as equerry. Now I wish to appoint him Constable of the Island of Sark. And his betrothed shall be lady-in-waiting to Dame de Carteret, until their wedding day arrives."

Van den Schreyer spoke for the first time since he had come into the hall.

"This girl delivered Sark; my sailors and I only helped her. All the jewels I found in the caves should go to her, too, and shall. I have been happy to serve her, without hope and without thought of reward; and to-morrow when I sail again for the West Indies, I shall take one very precious memory—of her sweet smile, and the joyful light in her eyes, now that she has found the one she loves."

ᛥ XXVIII ᛥ

A SUNNY day in October, a number of small
boats could be seen approaching the deserted
cliffs of Sark, still scarred by the fires of Buron's
vengeance. Sailing towards the Conchée the tide carried the little fleet towards Dixcart Bay. At last in
shallow water they came to anchor, and Sir Helier de
Carteret assisted his lady into the punt from which
she would disembark on the beach.

The surf was breaking into a border of white on
the sand when Lucas stepped out of the punt into the
water and humbly asked the honor, due to him as the
only Sark-born man present, to carry Dame de Carteret ashore. Then he returned through the surf to lift
his own beloved Guillette onto the soil of her native
Island.

Emotion too deep for words filled their hearts. They stood hand in hand, and Guillette's lovely face under her bridal coif was saddened for a moment by the memories this landing brought her. Married that morning at dawn in Jersey in the presence of Sir Helier and his lady, Lucas and Guillette were blissfully happy in the knowledge that they were to be the first of the forty families the newly created Seigneur of Sark was bringing from Jersey this autumn morning to receive grants of land and to settle in peace and security as farmers in Sark.

All stood in silence while Sir Helier, removing his casque, asked the blessing of God for the people who under the Queen's charter were to be the pioneers of a new order in Sark. He then addressed his little colony, bidding them hold close together and work always for the whole as one family. To each one who listened the words conjured up thoughts of past glory and courage, and filled them with resolution for the future. With one accord they raised their voices in the Te Deum.

Little by little the beach became covered with the goods and farm implements of the settlers. Cattle were swum ashore, symbols of peace and order, and gradually the people wound their way up the steep path from the shore—until only an old man was left hitching his oxen to his cart. At the top of the gulley the Seigneur looked down at the scene, and seeing the old man, he shouted, "Go on, *mon vieux,* you can work in peace. Sark is not accursed any more."

"There isn't any accursed island any more," repeated the peasant. Then after a long and thoughtful pause, he added, "From now on till judgment-day, God willing, people will call it the Fortunate Isle."

(2)